Christmas
COOKIES

Gingerbread
Snowflake Cookies
(page 44)

Christmas
COOKIES

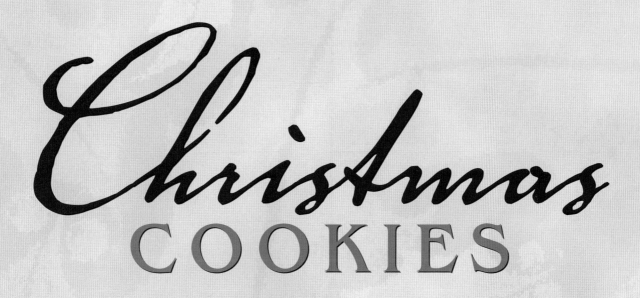

Christmas Cookies
©2006 by Oxmoor House, Inc.
Book Division of Southern Progress Corporation
P.O. Box 2262, Birmingham, AL 35201-2262

ISBN: 978-0-8487-3111-3
Printed and bound in Mexico

Cover: *Peppermint Patties (page 74)*
Back Cover: *Aunt Neal's Old-Fashioned Tea Cakes (page 28)*

Oxmoor House, Inc.
Editor in Chief: Nancy Fitzpatrick Wyatt
Executive Editor: Susan Carlisle Payne
Art Director: Cynthia Rose Cooper
Copy Chief: Allison Long Lowery

Christmas Cookies
Editor: Susan Hernandez Ray
Copy Editor: Donna Baldone
Assistant Editor: Terri Laschober
Editorial Assistants: Julie Boston, Shannon Friedmann
Contributing Designer: Carol Damsky
Test Kitchens Director: Elizabeth Tyler Austin
Assistant Test Kitchens Director: Julie Christopher
Test Kitchens Staff: Kristi Carter, Nicole Lee Faber,
Kathleen Royal Phillips, Elise Weis, Kelley Self Wilton
Senior Photographers: Ralph Anderson, Jim Bathie
Photographers: Tina Cornett, Brit Huckaby
Senior Photo Stylist: Kay E. Clarke
Contributing Photo Stylists: Virginia Cravens Houston,
Leslie Byars Simpson
Publishing Systems Administrator: Rick Tucker
Director of Production: Laura Lockhart
Production Manager: Greg A. Amason
Production Assistant: Faye Porter Bonner

CONTENTS

Making Memories 6

Cookie Primer 32

Shaped Cookies 36

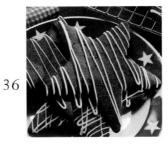

Drop Cookies 80

Bar Cookies 102

making memories

BAKING COOKIES WITH KIDS

Create special memories this Christmas season by enjoying time together in the kitchen.

There's just something magical about peering through the window of the oven door to see your creations begin to take shape. In fact, it's hard to wait for the cookies to finish baking to take that first warm bite. Kids love baking cookies and packaging them as gifts—or sharing their homemade treats with holiday visitors. Try making a classic with your kids such as Gingerbread People Cookies on the following page or the Braided Candy Canes on page 14. And enjoy your cookies with a cup of cocoa from page 12 or 13. The following tips will help your little elves get started with their Christmas baking.

Keys to Kids in the Kitchen:

• Always wash your hands before you begin.
• Put long hair up and don't wear baggy sleeves.
• Before cooking, read the recipe with your kids to make sure that everyone understands it. And be sure to follow the directions exactly.
• After you read the recipe, have the kids gather all the ingredients and arrange them together in the cooking area. After you use an item, have the kids put it away.
• Cooking is a great learning tool for teaching kids how to measure accurately. Show them how to spoon, not scoop, the flour into a dry measuring cup and level it with a knife.
• Use a glass measuring cup with pouring spout to measure liquids. Show them how to read the liquid measurement at eye level.
• Remind children that all cutting and chopping, and operation of the cooktop and oven should be done by a grown-up.
• Keep fingers away from electric mixer blades.
• Always use oven mitts when handling hot baking sheets and saucepans.
• Keep the handles of pots and pans turned away from the edges of the cooktop.

GINGERBREAD PEOPLE COOKIES

Prep: 35 minutes   Cook: 8 minutes per batch   Other: 1 hour

These little guys are almost too cute to eat. Save a few to scatter among holiday decorations for a centerpiece.

2¼ cups all-purpose flour

½ teaspoon baking powder

¼ teaspoon baking soda

¼ teaspoon salt

1½ teaspoons ground ginger

1 teaspoon ground cinnamon

¼ teaspoon ground nutmeg

¼ teaspoon ground cloves

6 tablespoons granulated sugar

¼ cup butter, softened

½ cup molasses

1 large egg white

2 tablespoons dried currants

1¼ cups powdered sugar

2 tablespoons lemon juice

¼ teaspoon vanilla extract

Stir together first 8 ingredients in a bowl; set aside.

Combine granulated sugar and butter in a large bowl; beat at medium speed with an electric mixer 5 minutes. Add molasses and egg white; beat well. Add flour mixture to sugar mixture; beat at low speed until well blended. Divide dough in half, and shape each half into a ball; wrap in plastic wrap. Chill 1 hour.

Working with 1 portion at a time (keep remaining dough in refrigerator), roll each portion to ⅛-inch thickness on a heavily floured surface; cut with a 2½-inch boy or girl cookie cutter. Place gingerbread cookies 1 inch apart on lightly greased baking sheets. Arrange currants on cookies as eyes and buttons.

Bake at 350° for 8 minutes or until lightly browned. Remove to wire racks to cool completely.

Combine powdered sugar, lemon juice, and vanilla in a small bowl. Spoon into a decorating bag or zip-top freezer bag. Snip a tiny hole in 1 corner of bag, and decorate cookies as desired. Yield: 4 dozen.

OLD-FASHIONED HOT COCOA
Prep: 2 minutes   Cook: 5 minutes

Create warm memories by serving a mug of steamy cocoa with your favorite cookies.

$^1/_3$ cup sugar

$^1/_4$ cup unsweetened cocoa

Pinch of salt

$^1/_2$ cup water

4 cups milk

$^1/_4$ teaspoon vanilla extract

Marshmallows (optional)

Combine first 4 ingredients in a heavy saucepan; bring to a boil over medium heat, stirring constantly. Stir in milk, and heat thoroughly (do not boil). Stir in vanilla. Serve cocoa immediately with marshmallows, if desired. Yield: 4$^1/_2$ cups.

Hot Cinnamon Cocoa: Stir 1 teaspoon ground cinnamon into saucepan with first 4 ingredients. Proceed as directed.

HOT CHOCOLATE MIX

Prep: 5 minutes

Make a batch of this mix to enjoy during the holiday season,
or package it to share with friends.

1 (9.6-ounce) package nonfat dry
   milk
4 cups miniature marshmallows

1 1/2 cups powdered sugar
1 cup unsweetened cocoa

Stir together all ingredients in a large bowl.
Store chocolate mixture in an airtight container at room temperature. Yield: 14 servings.

Hot Chocolate: Stir 1/2 cup Hot Chocolate Mix into 1 cup hot milk. Serve Hot Chocolate immediately. Yield: 1 serving.

BRAIDED CANDY CANES
Prep: 28 minutes   Cook: 15 minutes per batch

*You can also shape this dough into wreaths and attach
red cinnamon candies as holly berries.*

³/₄ cup butter, softened
1 cup granulated sugar
3 large eggs
1 tablespoon vanilla extract
4 cups all-purpose flour

1 tablespoon baking powder
¹/₂ teaspoon baking soda
1 egg white, lightly beaten
Red decorator sugar crystals

Beat butter at medium speed with an electric mixer until creamy; gradually add 1 cup sugar, beating well. Add eggs and vanilla, beating until blended.

Combine flour, baking powder, and soda; gradually add flour mixture to butter mixture, beating at low speed just until blended after each addition. Divide dough into fourths. Divide each portion into 14 pieces; shape each piece into a 9-inch rope. Fold ropes in half, and twist.

Shape twists into candy canes; brush with egg white, and sprinkle with decorator sugar crystals. Place cookies 2 inches apart on ungreased baking sheets.

Bake at 350° for 15 minutes or until edges begin to brown. Remove to wire racks to cool completely. Yield: 4¹/₂ dozen.

BRAIDED
CANDY
CANES

SHARING WITH FRIENDS

Enjoy an afternoon of fun with friends—whether it's baking cookies together as the main attraction or everyone baking them at home and bringing them to a party, potluck style.

Christmas, cookies, and camaraderie just naturally go together. So invite some friends over for a few hours of holiday baking. Laughter and fun are the two key ingredients. Select three or four favorite cookie recipes, and split the cost of the ingredients. Be sure to provide containers for guests to take home a portion of each batch for nibbling and gift giving.

If you're not set up for a group in your kitchen, have friends over for a cookie swap. A cookie swap can be as formal or as casual as you like. You can serve a sit-down lunch; a buffet-style meal; or just coffee, tea, and milk to complement the cookies.

Whichever you choose, a baking party or a cookie swap, you'll enjoy an afternoon of fun with friends—and batches of cookies throughout the season.

Bake and Take Party

• Send a blank recipe card with the invitation and ask each friend to send back her favorite cookie recipe. That way, you can take turns making everyone's specialty.

• Make cookie dough ahead and chill or freeze it until you're ready to slice and bake.

• Make personalized aprons for each guest, or purchase white aprons and personalize them with paint pens.

• Divide your kitchen into stations—one for rolling and cutting dough and one for icing and decorating.

• Let cookies cool completely before packaging them. Provide sturdy containers and wraps for guests to package their goodies for the trip home. Baskets work well, as do decorated tins or simple boxes. Line the containers with greaseproof paper such as parchment, wax paper, or aluminum foil.

Cookie Swap Strategy

• Choose a theme, and carry it out in the invitations and with a take-home recipe booklet. For example, you could use star-shaped sugar cookies as a recurring motif for your party.

• Include a blank recipe card with the invitation so that you can compile a cookie swap

Glazed Sugar Cookies,
page 18

recipe booklet after the party. Encourage everyone to include a sentence or two with the recipe explaining its origin. This way, you'll not only be sharing cookies but also time-honored traditions.

• As the hostess, you'll want to make your cookies ahead so you'll be free to set the table, arrange the seating, and prepare the beverages.

• Make your cookies the centerpiece by displaying them on a decorated tiered tray, or decorate a small tree with cookie cutters.

• Provide cookie containers for each person to take their cookies home.

• Take turns hosting the party each year. Let a guest at your cookie swap volunteer to host the next one, or draw a name from the list of this year's guests, and designate her as the hostess for the next exchange.

• After the party, assemble the guests' cookie recipes in a booklet, and mail one to all of those who attended.

GLAZED SUGAR COOKIES
Prep: 30 minutes   Cook: 8 minutes per batch   Other: 1 hour

Pictured on previous page.

1 cup butter, softened
1 cup sugar
1 large egg
1 teaspoon vanilla extract
3 cups all-purpose flour

$^1/_4$ teaspoon salt
Glaze
Royal Icing
Edible gold dust
Clear vanilla extract

Beat butter and sugar at medium speed with an electric mixer until fluffy. Add egg and 1 teaspoon vanilla, beating until blended. Gradually add flour and salt, beating just until blended. Divide dough in half; cover and chill 1 hour.

Roll each portion of dough to $^1/_4$-inch thickness on a lightly floured surface. Cut dough into desired shapes with a $3^1/_2$-inch cutter; place on lightly greased baking sheets.

Bake at 350° for 8 minutes or until edges are lightly browned. Remove to wire racks to cool. Dip cookies in Glaze; place on wax paper to dry. Decorate with Royal Icing.

Combine $^1/_4$ teaspoon gold dust and $^1/_4$ teaspoon clear vanilla extract with a small paintbrush. Working quickly, brush on gold accents; add 1 drop clear vanilla at a time, as needed, to moisten gold dust. Sprinkle on more gold dust, if desired. Yield: 16 cookies.

Note: Cookies can also be cut with a $2^1/_2$-inch cutter. Decorator sugar crystals can be substituted for gold dust mixture. Yield: 3 dozen.

Glaze:
1 (16-ounce) package powdered sugar
4 to 6 tablespoons hot water

Whisk until blended and smooth. Yield: $1^1/_3$ cups.

Royal Icing:
1 (16-ounce) package powdered sugar
3 tablespoons meringue powder
6 tablespoons hot water
Liquid food coloring (optional)

Stir together first 3 ingredients until smooth. Stir in food coloring, if desired. Pour into a decorating bag or a large zip-top freezer bag. Snip a tiny hole in 1 corner of bag, and decorate as desired. Yield: about 3 cups.

CRISPY PEANUT BUTTER-CHOCOLATE TREATS
Prep: 15 minutes   Cook: 5 minutes

Kids will love these crisp cereal bars gone chocolate and made into lollipops.

1½ cups sugar
1½ cups light corn syrup
1½ cups chunky peanut butter

6 cups crisp rice cereal
1 (12-ounce) package semisweet
   chocolate morsels (2 cups)

Cook first 3 ingredients in a large saucepan over medium-low heat, stirring constantly, until blended and mixture begins to bubble. Remove from heat.

Combine cereal and chocolate morsels in a large bowl. Stir in hot peanut butter mixture until combined. Spread mixture into a 13- x 9-inch pan lined with plastic wrap.

Cool completely. Lift out of pan. Cut into stars or other shapes, using 2-inch cookie cutters, or cut into squares. Yield: 22 stars or 16 squares.

Note: To make lollipops, insert 4-inch paper craft sticks into cutouts.

serve with milk

serve with milk

serve with milk

serve with milk

Easy
Oatmeal - Chocolate Chip
Cookies
~Jan

EASY OATMEAL-CHOCOLATE CHIP COOKIES

Prep: 20 minutes   Cook: 10 minutes per batch

This is an easy recipe because you don't have to beat butter or shortening;
you just dump and stir ingredients in a big bowl.

2 cups all-purpose flour

1 teaspoon baking soda

½ teaspoon baking powder

½ teaspoon salt

2 cups uncooked quick-cooking oats

1 cup granulated sugar

1 cup firmly packed light brown
   sugar

1 cup chopped pecans

1 (6-ounce) package semisweet
   chocolate morsels (1 cup)

1 cup vegetable oil

2 large eggs, lightly beaten

1 teaspoon vanilla extract

Stir together first 9 ingredients in a large bowl. Add oil, eggs, and vanilla; stir well. Shape into 1-inch balls (dough will be crumbly). Place balls on ungreased baking sheets.

Bake at 350° for 10 minutes or until golden. Let cool on baking sheets 1 minute. Remove to wire racks to cool completely. Yield: 6 dozen.

BASIC SHORTBREAD
Prep: 18 minutes   Cook: 50 minutes

Shortbread is made with a few basic ingredients, and the results are sensational.
The key to success with this thick shortbread is baking it slowly so that it doesn't brown.

1 cup butter, softened
½ cup sugar
¼ teaspoon vanilla extract

2¼ cups unbleached all-purpose
   flour
⅛ teaspoon salt

Beat butter at medium speed with an electric mixer until creamy; gradually add sugar, beating well. Stir in vanilla.

Combine flour and salt; gradually add to butter mixture, beating at low speed until blended.

Roll dough to ½-inch thickness on a lightly floured surface. Cut with a 2½-inch round cutter or Christmas cookie cutter. Place 2 inches apart on an ungreased baking sheet.

Bake at 275° for 50 minutes or until bottoms begin to brown. Cool 2 minutes on baking sheet; remove to a wire rack to cool completely. Yield: 1 dozen.

Note: Unbleached flour is the best-quality, freshest flour for baking and is particularly good in simple recipes such as shortbread. All-purpose flour works fine in this recipe, too.

WRAPPING COOKIES WITH LOVE

Turn your kitchen into Santa's workshop, and bundle batches of cookies to give to friends and neighbors. Many times the package can be as inviting as the cookies inside.

Cookies wrapped in creative containers are a welcome treat at Christmastime or anytime. Search flea markets, discount stores, and kitchen shops throughout the year for clever packaging supplies. Collect ribbons, trims, and other wrapping materials to put together pretty holiday bundles. Let our cookie-packaging ideas here and on the following pages inspire you to get started early on some holiday baking. Look for recipes and more wraps throughout the book.

Cookie Gifts

• Organize sturdy cookies such as shortbread into little stacks; tie them with colored raffia, jute, or heavy twine, and nestle them in small decorative boxes. Trim each box with ribbon.

• Bundle cookies in small plastic bags and place them inside tea cups or coffee mugs.

• Purchase square bakery boxes from the supermarket, line them with colorful waxed tissue, and fill them with an assortment of baked goodies. Add a homemade gift tag for an extra-special touch.

• Use your computer to design and print the recipes for your cookies to include with gift packages. Roll up the printed sheets, and tie with ribbon, twine, or raffia.

• How can you get it all done? Bake and freeze cookies up to 3 months in advance. Be sure to double-wrap the cookies securely, and write the date and type of cookie on the package. When you're ready to assemble your gifts, just let the cookies come to room temperature. You can also freeze most cookie dough up to 3 months ahead. Let it thaw in the refrigerator before baking.

PRETTY PACKAGING IDEAS

◀ Christmas Cookie Canister Empty a canister. Wrap canister and lid with white paper, and tape or glue seams. Then wrap the white canister with toile waxed tissue paper, and tape or glue the seams. Or forego the white paper and toile tissue, and wrap the canister in holiday wrapping paper. Fill canister with Aunt Neal's Old-Fashioned Tea Cakes (recipe on page 28), and replace lid. Tie ribbon around canister, and add a gift tag.

◀ Out of the Box Place Fudgy Peppermint Candy Brownies (recipe on page 29) in a tissue-lined box such as this monogrammed box. Close box and tie with decorative ribbon. Be sure to enclose a gift card.

Wrap and Roll Package Double Chocolate ▶ Chews (recipe on page 31) in parchment paper with the recipe written on the outside. Tie each end with pretty holiday ribbon.

◀ Stacked with Style Stack Sugar Crinkles (recipe on page 30) inside of net fabric. Tie the packages with coordinating ribbon, and tuck the pretty stacks inside a tin or a clear plastic bag to keep cookies fresh.

AUNT NEAL'S OLD-FASHIONED TEA CAKES
Prep: 17 minutes   Cook: 8 minutes per batch   Other: 1 hour

These delicious tea cakes (pictured on page 26) were made by an Aunt Cornelia ("Neal") on special occasions and holidays, using hand-churned butter and eggs she gathered from the hen-house. This southern Georgia version dates back to the turn of the twentieth century.

1 cup butter, softened	1 teaspoon baking powder
1 cup granulated sugar	½ teaspoon baking soda
1 large egg, lightly beaten	½ teaspoon salt
1 teaspoon vanilla extract	½ cup milk
3 cups all-purpose flour	White sparkling sugar

Beat butter at medium speed with an electric mixer until creamy; gradually add 1 cup sugar, beating well. Add egg and vanilla; beat well.

Combine flour and next 3 ingredients; add to butter mixture alternately with milk, beginning and ending with flour mixture. Mix at low speed after each addition just until blended. Shape dough into 2 discs.

Wrap in wax paper, and chill at least 1 hour. Roll each disc to ¼-inch thickness on a floured surface. Cut with a 3½-inch round cutter; place 1 inch apart on lightly greased baking sheets. Sprinkle with sparkling sugar.

Bake at 400° for 7 to 8 minutes or until edges are lightly browned. Cool 1 minute on baking sheets; remove to wire racks to cool completely. Yield: 2 dozen.

FUDGY PEPPERMINT CANDY BROWNIES

Prep: 17 minutes   Cook: 45½ minutes

These dense brownies (pictured on page 26) are for the true chocolate-mint lover. The crunchy crumb crust is topped with a fudgy mint brownie and frosted with melted chocolate-peppermint candies.

1½ cups chocolate wafer crumbs
⅓ cup finely chopped pecans, toasted
⅓ cup butter or margarine, melted
10 chocolate-covered peppermint patties, chopped (we tested with York®)
½ cup butter or margarine
3 (1-ounce) unsweetened chocolate baking squares

1 cup sugar
2 large eggs, lightly beaten
½ teaspoon vanilla extract
½ teaspoon peppermint extract (not flavoring)
½ cup all-purpose flour
⅛ teaspoon salt
14 chocolate-covered peppermint patties, halved

Line a 9-inch square pan with foil, allowing foil to extend over ends of pan; grease foil. Stir together first 3 ingredients; press into pan. Bake at 350° for 10 minutes. Sprinkle chopped peppermint patties over warm crust.

While crust is baking, combine ½ cup butter and chocolate squares in a glass bowl. Microwave at HIGH 1 minute or until butter melts; stir until chocolate melts and mixture is smooth. Stir in sugar, eggs, vanilla, and peppermint extract. Add flour and salt; stir well. Pour over crust.

Bake at 350° for 33 minutes. Remove from oven, and immediately sprinkle with halved peppermint patties. Bake 2½ more minutes. Remove from oven, and let cool 1 minute.

Spread and swirl softened peppermint patties over brownies. (Don't wait too long before swirling or candy may be too firm to spread.) Cool completely in pan on a wire rack. Lift brownies out of pan, and cut into squares. Yield: 2½ dozen.

SUGAR CRINKLES

Prep: 15 minutes   Cook: 9 minutes per batch   Other: 1 hour

Your kitchen will smell like a bakery when you make these
tender treasures (pictured on page 27).

1 cup shortening
1½ cups sugar
2 large eggs
1 teaspoon lemon extract
1 teaspoon vanilla extract

2½ cups all-purpose flour
2 teaspoons baking powder
½ teaspoon salt
¼ cup sugar

Beat shortening and 1½ cups sugar at medium speed with an electric mixer until fluffy. Add eggs and flavorings, beating until blended.

Combine flour, baking powder, and salt; gradually add to shortening mixture, beating well. Cover and chill dough at least 1 hour.

Shape dough into 1-inch balls. Roll balls in ¼ cup sugar. Place balls on ungreased baking sheets.

Bake at 350° for 8 to 9 minutes or until barely golden. Let cool 2 minutes on baking sheets. Remove to wire racks to cool completely. Yield: about 5½ dozen.

DOUBLE CHOCOLATE CHEWS

Prep: 25 minutes   Cook: 8 minutes per batch

Chocolate lovers on your gift list will rave about these rich cookies (pictured on page 27).

1 (6-ounce) package semisweet
    chocolate morsels (1 cup),
    divided
3 tablespoons vegetable oil
$1^3/_4$ cups all-purpose flour
$^2/_3$ cup sifted powdered sugar
$^1/_3$ cup unsweetened cocoa
$2^1/_4$ teaspoons baking powder

$^1/_8$ teaspoon salt
1 cup firmly packed light brown
    sugar
3 tablespoons light corn syrup
2 tablespoons water
$2^1/_2$ teaspoons vanilla extract
1 large egg

Heat $^3/_4$ cup chocolate morsels and oil in a small saucepan over low heat, stirring constantly, until chocolate melts. Pour mixture into a large bowl, and cool 5 minutes.

Stir together flour and next 4 ingredients until blended.

Stir brown sugar and next 4 ingredients into chocolate mixture; stir in flour mixture and remaining $^1/_4$ cup morsels. (Dough will be stiff.)

Drop dough by level tablespoonfuls 2 inches apart onto lightly greased baking sheets.

Bake at 350° for 8 minutes. Cool on baking sheets 2 minutes; remove to wire racks to cool completely. Yield: $2^1/_2$ dozen.

COOKIE
primer

Follow these tips for measuring, rolling, cutting, baking, and decorating flawless cookies every time.

◀ Use stainless steel or plastic measuring cups to measure dry ingredients. For flour, lightly spoon into cup, letting it mound slightly; then level the top (shown at right).

When measuring dry ▶ ingredients, level the top, using the straight edge of a spatula or knife.

To measure brown sugar ▶ accurately, use the measuring cup that holds the exact amount called for in a recipe. Pack brown sugar firmly into dry measuring cup; then level the top.

Butter, margarine, and shortening are all available as sticks marked in tablespoon increments for easy measuring. Use a knife and be exact in cutting just the right amount needed for a recipe.

◀ Measure liquids in a glass or clear plastic measuring cup with a spout. Read liquid measurements at eye level.

Roll cookie dough to an even and ▶ precise thickness using rubber rolling pin rings. Or use a ruler to check thickness of dough after rolling.

Punch cookie cutter quickly ▶ into dough, and promptly remove cutter. Make cutouts close together to get maximum yield from dough.

A tip from cookie baking pros: Once you've rolled and cut cookies and placed them on baking sheets, place baking sheets in the refrigerator or freezer 5 to 10 minutes to help set the shape before baking.

Dip cookie cutter in flour between cutouts to prevent sticking. ▼

Use a wide spatula or dough ▶ scraper to transfer dough cutouts to baking sheet. Place cutouts several inches apart on baking sheet to allow for spreading during baking.

◀ If you don't have cookie cutters handy, use a fluted pastry wheel to cut out cookie "sticks."

Use Royal Icing (recipe ▶ on page 18) to define and decorate your cookies.

Cookies are easy to transfer ▶ to wire racks when you bake them on parchment paper-lined baking sheets. And cleanup's easy, too!

When making drop cookies, spoon dough evenly onto baking sheet as specific recipes direct. A cookie scoop easily measures tablespoon portions. Otherwise, use two spoons—one to scoop the dough, the other to push the dough off the spoon onto the baking sheet. ▼

◀ To make sandwich cookies with a window, use two sizes of the same cutter. Bake some solid cookies and some cutout cookies. Spread chocolate or your favorite jam on the solid cookies; top with cutout cookies.

Use decorative cutters ▶ to cut out shapes from a pan of fudgy brownies. Just line the pan with foil before baking; then lift uncut baked brownies from pan and cut out shapes.

- Cool cookies completely before storing.

- Separate moist or sticky cookies with layers of wax paper.

- Store soft cookies in an airtight container. If cookies harden, soften them again by placing an apple wedge on a piece of wax paper in the container. (Be sure to remove the apple after one day.)

- Store crisp cookies in a container with a loose-fitting lid.

- Double-bag cookies in zip-top freezer bags for freezing. For crisp cookies, bring to room temperature; then reheat at 325° for 3 to 5 minutes.

◀ Make ice cream sandwiches using cookie cutters. Bake a batch of cookies using a 3-inch round cutter to shape them; then spread 3 to 4 cups of ice cream in a plastic wrap-lined 9-inch cakepan, and freeze. Unmold ice cream, and use the same cutter to cut out circles. Assemble sandwiches.

COLORING SUGAR

You can color your own sugar by stirring together 1 cup granulated sugar and 5 drops liquid food coloring. Let dry, and store in an airtight container. Use colored sugar to decorate holiday cookies.

Use various shapes and ▶ sizes of cookie cutters to cut out bread for shapely French toast or party tea sandwiches.

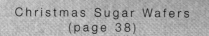

Christmas Sugar Wafers
(page 38)

shaped cookies

CHRISTMAS SUGAR WAFERS
Prep: 32 minutes   Cook: 8 minutes per batch   Other: 20 minutes

Freezing the dough before cutting makes these cookies crunchy (pictured on page 36).

6 tablespoons granulated sugar
¼ cup butter
2 tablespoons firmly packed dark
    brown sugar
1½ teaspoons vanilla extract
2 large egg whites
1½ cups all-purpose flour
3 tablespoons cornstarch

½ teaspoon baking powder
¼ teaspoon baking soda
¼ teaspoon salt
1 cup powdered sugar
2½ teaspoons warm water
1 teaspoon light corn syrup
¼ teaspoon vanilla extract
Dash of salt

Combine first 3 ingredients in a large bowl; beat at medium speed with an electric mixer until well blended (about 5 minutes). Beat in 1½ teaspoons vanilla. Add egg whites, 1 at a time, beating well after each addition.

Combine flour and next 4 ingredients, stirring well with a whisk. Add to butter mixture; beat well. Turn dough out onto a lightly floured surface (dough will be soft). Divide dough into 4 equal portions. Roll each portion into an 8-inch circle between 2 sheets of plastic wrap. Freeze dough 20 minutes or until plastic wrap can be removed easily.

Working with 1 portion of dough at a time (keep remaining dough in freezer), remove top sheet of plastic wrap. Cut dough with a 3-inch cookie cutter, dipping cutter in flour between each use; place cookies on lightly greased baking sheets. Discard bottom sheet of plastic wrap; reserve remaining dough scraps. Repeat procedure with remaining dough.

Gently gather reserved dough into a ball; repeat rolling, freezing, and cutting.

Bake at 375° for 8 minutes or until cookies are lightly browned. Remove to wire racks to cool completely.

Combine 1 cup powdered sugar and remaining ingredients in a small bowl; stir with a fork until combined. Drizzle icing over cookies, or spoon into a small zip-top freezer bag; cut a tiny hole in 1 corner of bag, and pipe designs onto cookies. Yield: 2 dozen.

SOUR CREAM-NUTMEG SUGAR COOKIES

Prep: 25 minutes   Cook: 12 minutes per batch   Other: 1 hour

*These fragrant, buttery cutouts are soft and thick like old-fashioned
tea cakes your grandmother used to bake.*

1 cup butter, softened
1½ cups sugar
2 large eggs
1 cup sour cream
1½ teaspoons vanilla extract
4½ cups all-purpose flour

1 teaspoon baking powder
1 teaspoon baking soda
1 teaspoon salt
½ teaspoon ground nutmeg
Sugar

Beat butter at medium speed with an electric mixer until creamy; gradually add 1½ cups sugar, beating well. Add eggs, beating well. Add sour cream and vanilla, beating well.

Combine flour and next 4 ingredients; gradually add to butter mixture, beating well. Cover and chill at least 1 hour.

Divide dough into fourths. Working with 1 portion of dough at a time (keep remaining dough in refrigerator), roll each portion to ¼-inch thickness on a lightly floured surface. Cut with a 3-inch cookie cutter; place on ungreased baking sheets. Sprinkle cookies with additional sugar.

Bake at 375° for 12 minutes or until lightly browned. Cool slightly on baking sheets; remove to wire racks to cool completely. Yield: 4 dozen.

CHOCOLATE STAR COOKIES

Prep: 40 minutes   Cook: 10 minutes per batch   Other: 1 hour

These soft and chewy cookies make a delicious treat anytime of year.

1½ cups butter, softened
2½ cups sifted powdered sugar
2 large eggs
1 teaspoon vanilla extract
3 cups all-purpose flour

1 cup Dutch process cocoa
¼ teaspoon salt
½ teaspoon ground cinnamon
2 (2-ounce) vanilla bark coating
      squares

Beat butter at medium speed with an electric mixer until creamy; gradually add powdered sugar, beating well. Add eggs and vanilla; beat until blended.

Combine flour and next 3 ingredients. Gradually add flour mixture to butter mixture, beating at low speed until blended. Divide dough in half; wrap each dough portion tightly in plastic wrap. Chill at least 1 hour.

Roll 1 portion at a time to ¼-inch thickness on a floured surface. Cut with a 4-inch star-shaped cutter; place on ungreased baking sheets.

Bake at 350° for 10 minutes; remove to wire racks to cool completely.

Place bark coating in a small zip-top freezer bag; seal. Submerge in hot water until coating melts. Snip a tiny hole in 1 corner of bag, and drizzle over cookies. Yield: 2 dozen.

JAM KOLACHES
Prep: 16 minutes   Cook: 15 minutes per batch

There's a strawberry surprise in the center of each cookie.

½ cup butter, softened
1 (3-ounce) package cream
    cheese, softened

1¼ cups all-purpose flour
About ½ cup strawberry jam
¼ cup sifted powdered sugar

Beat butter and cream cheese at medium speed with an electric mixer until creamy. Add flour to butter mixture, beating well.

Roll dough to ⅛-inch thickness on a lightly floured surface; cut with a 2½-inch round cookie cutter. Place on lightly greased baking sheets. Spoon ¼ teaspoon jam on each cookie; fold opposite sides to center, slightly overlapping edges.

Bake at 375° for 15 minutes. Remove to wire racks to cool; sprinkle with powdered sugar. Yield: 3½ dozen.

SPECULAAS

Prep: 22 minutes   Cook: 25 minutes per batch

*These heavily spiced cookies baked in wooden cookie molds are part of the
Dutch tradition of St. Nicholas Day, celebrated December 6 in Holland. The night before,
children leave carrots in their shoes for the saint's horse; in the morning, they find treats, often
speculaas, in place of the carrots.*

1   cup butter, softened
¾   cup firmly packed brown sugar
1   large egg
¼   teaspoon anise extract or
      ½ teaspoon anise seeds, crushed
⅛   teaspoon almond extract
3   cups all-purpose flour
1   tablespoon baking powder
Pinch of salt
2   teaspoons ground cinnamon

¾   teaspoon ground cloves
¼   teaspoon ground nutmeg
¼   teaspoon unsweetened cocoa
¼   teaspoon pepper
½   teaspoon grated lemon or
      orange rind
¼   cup finely chopped blanched
      almonds
1   (6-ounce) can whole natural
      almonds

Beat butter at medium speed with an electric mixer until creamy; gradually add brown sugar, beating well. Add egg, anise extract, and almond extract, beating well.

Combine flour and next 8 ingredients; stir well. Add to butter mixture, beating at low speed until blended. Stir in chopped almonds.

Divide dough in half. Shape 1 portion of dough into a ball; knead 3 or 4 times until smooth. Roll dough into a 9-inch square on a lightly greased baking sheet. Press onto floured cookie molds, or cut dough into 36 (1½-inch) squares (do not separate cookies). Press a whole almond into center of each square. Repeat procedure with remaining dough.

Bake at 325° for 25 minutes. Cool slightly on baking sheets; remove cookies to wire racks to cool completely. Break cookies apart, and store in airtight containers. Yield: 6 dozen.

GINGERBREAD SNOWFLAKE COOKIES
Prep: 1 hour, 10 minutes   Cook: 12 minutes per batch   Other: 1 hour

Royal Icing dries rapidly. Work quickly, keeping extra icing covered tightly at all times.

1 cup butter or margarine, softened
1 cup granulated sugar
¼ cup water
1½ teaspoons baking soda
1 cup molasses
5 cups all-purpose flour
¼ teaspoon salt

1½ tablespoons ground ginger
1½ teaspoons ground cinnamon
½ teaspoon ground allspice
Royal Icing
White sparkling sugar (optional)
Powdered sugar (optional)

Beat butter and 1 cup sugar at medium speed with an electric mixer until fluffy (3 to 4 minutes). Stir together ¼ cup water and soda until dissolved; stir in molasses. Combine flour and next 4 ingredients. Add to butter mixture alternately with molasses mixture, beginning and ending with flour mixture. Shape into a ball; cover and chill 1 hour.

Roll to ¼-inch thickness on a lightly floured surface. Cut with a 5½-inch snowflake cookie cutter. Place 2 inches apart on parchment paper-lined baking sheets. Poke holes in snowflakes, using a plastic drinking straw, if desired. Bake at 350° for 12 minutes. Cool 1 minute on baking sheets; remove to wire racks to cool completely.

Spoon Royal Icing into a small zip-top freezer bag. Snip a tiny hole in 1 corner of bag, and decorate cookies. If desired, sprinkle icing with sparkling sugar or plain cookies with powdered sugar. Yield: 21 cookies.

Royal Icing:
Prep: 5 minutes

1 (16-ounce) package powdered sugar
3 tablespoons meringue powder
5 to 6 tablespoons warm water
1 teaspoon light corn syrup

Beat all ingredients at medium-low speed with an electric mixer 5 to 7 minutes or until stiff peaks form. Yield: 1⅔ cups.

Note: Sparkling sugar and meringue powder can be found at kitchen shops.

ROSEMARY SHORTBREAD COOKIES

Prep: 15 minutes   Cook: 20 minutes

*Temptingly flavored with fragrant rosemary, these wonderfully tender-crisp cookies
are perfect with a cup of your favorite hot tea or atop a scoop of sherbet.*

½ cup butter, softened
⅓ cup sifted powdered sugar
1½ cups all-purpose flour

2 tablespoons minced fresh
   rosemary

Beat butter at medium speed with an electric mixer until creamy; gradually add sugar, beating well.

Gradually add flour to butter mixture, beating at low speed until blended. Gently stir in rosemary.

Roll dough to ¼-inch thickness on a floured surface. Cut with a 2-inch cookie cutter; place cutouts on lightly greased baking sheets.

Bake at 325° for 18 to 20 minutes or until edges are lightly browned. Remove to wire rack to cool completely. Yield: 1 dozen.

BROWN SUGAR COOKIES
Prep: 28 minutes   Cook: 12 minutes per batch

When butter and dark brown sugar blend and bake,
the result is crisp praline-tasting cookies.

1 cup butter, softened
1½ cups firmly packed dark brown
    sugar
1 large egg
1 teaspoon vanilla extract

3⅓ cups all-purpose flour
1 teaspoon baking soda
½ teaspoon salt
Decorator sugar crystals

Beat butter at medium speed with an electric mixer until creamy. Gradually add brown sugar, beating well. Add egg and vanilla, beating well.

Combine flour, soda, and salt; add to butter mixture, beating just until blended.

Roll dough to ¼-inch thickness between 2 sheets of wax paper. Cut with 4-inch cookie cutters. Place 1 inch apart on ungreased baking sheets. Sprinkle cookies with decorator sugar crystals.

Bake at 350° for 10 to 12 minutes or until golden. Let cookies cool 1 minute on baking sheets; carefully remove to wire racks to cool completely. Yield: about 2½ dozen.

CINNAMON COOKIES
Prep: 25 minutes   Cook: 25 minutes

These fragrant cookies will make a tasty homemade gift for everyone on your Christmas list.

¾ cup butter, softened

1 cup sugar

1 egg yolk

2 cups all-purpose flour

---

1 tablespoon ground cinnamon

3 cups finely chopped pecans

Beat first 3 ingredients at medium speed with an electric mixer 2 to 3 minutes or until light and fluffy. Add flour and cinnamon, beating well. (Dough will be stiff.)

Roll dough to ⅛-inch thickness between 2 sheets of parchment paper. Remove top sheet of parchment, and invert dough onto a lightly greased baking sheet. Remove parch-ment paper, and press pecans evenly into dough.

Bake cookies at 350° for 15 minutes; reduce heat to 250°, and bake 10 more min-utes. Remove from oven, and immediately cut cookies (while dough is hot) into 3- x 1½-inch rectangles, using a pizza cut-ter. Cool on a wire rack. Yield: 3 dozen.

Note: Sprinkle any cookie crumbs that

PEPPERMINT CANDY SHORTBREAD
Prep: 45 minutes   Cook: 25 minutes per batch

Sprinkle crushed hard peppermint candy on these vanilla-dipped shortbread triangles.

1 cup butter, softened
⅓ cup sugar
2½ cups all-purpose flour
4 (2-ounce) vanilla bark coating
     squares

⅔ cup crushed hard peppermint
    candy

Beat butter at medium speed with an electric mixer until creamy; gradually add sugar, beating well. Add flour, beating just until blended.

Divide dough into 3 equal portions. Place 1 portion of dough on an ungreased baking sheet; roll into a 6-inch circle. Score dough into 8 triangles. Repeat procedure with remaining 2 portions of dough.

Bake at 325° for 25 minutes or until barely golden. Let cool on baking sheets 5 minutes. Remove to wire racks to cool completely. Working very carefully, separate discs into wedges. (Shortbread is very fragile. Be gentle with it so tips remain intact.)

Melt bark coating in top of a double boiler over hot water. Remove from heat. Carefully dip wide edges of shortbread in melted coating; place shortbread on wax paper. Sprinkle crushed candy over coated edges. Let stand until coating is firm. Yield: 2 dozen.

ORANGE-DATE-NUT COOKIES

Prep: 40 minutes   Cook: 10 minutes per batch   Other: 2 hours

Here's a great gift to mail—or to keep and enjoy with hot orange tea.

1 (10-ounce) package chopped
    dates
1 teaspoon grated orange rind
1 tablespoon orange juice
1 cup butter or margarine,
    softened
1½ cups sugar

1 large egg
1 teaspoon vanilla extract
2½ cups all-purpose flour
1½ teaspoons baking powder
½ teaspoon salt
1 cup finely chopped toasted
    pecans, divided

Line a 9- x 5-inch loafpan with aluminum foil, allowing foil to extend over edges of pan. Set aside.

Position knife blade in food processor bowl; add first 3 ingredients. Process 45 seconds or until dates are finely chopped.

Beat butter at medium speed with a heavy-duty electric stand mixer until blended. Gradually add sugar, beating until blended. Add egg and vanilla; beat well.

Combine flour, baking powder, and salt; gradually add to butter mixture, beating at low speed just until blended.

Divide dough into 3 portions. Knead ½ cup pecans into 1 portion of dough; press into prepared pan. Knead date mixture into 1 portion of dough; press in pan over pecan dough. Knead remaining ½ cup pecans into remaining dough; press into pan over date dough. Cover and chill at least 2 hours.

Invert loafpan onto a cutting board; remove and discard aluminum foil. Cut dough lengthwise into 4 sections. Cut each section of dough crosswise into ¼-inch slices. Place slices 1½ inches apart on lightly greased baking sheets.

Bake at 350° for 9 to 10 minutes or until lightly browned. Cool slightly on baking sheets; remove to wire racks to cool completely. Yield: 8 dozen.

NEAPOLITAN COOKIES

Prep: 20 minutes   Cook: 10 minutes per batch   Other: 8 hours

The ultimate make-ahead cookies, these holiday classics can be frozen up to a month ahead.

1   cup butter or margarine,
       softened
1   cup sugar
1   large egg
1   teaspoon vanilla extract
2½ cups all-purpose flour
1½ teaspoons baking powder
½   teaspoon salt
1   (1-ounce) unsweetened chocolate
       baking square, melted

⅓   cup finely chopped walnuts
       or pecans
¼   cup finely chopped candied
       cherries
1   or 2 drops red liquid food
       coloring
⅓   cup flaked coconut
½   teaspoon rum extract

Beat butter at medium speed with an electric mixer until creamy. Add sugar, beating until light and fluffy. Add egg and vanilla, beating until blended. Gradually add flour, baking powder, and salt, beating until mixture is blended.

Divide dough into thirds; place each portion in a separate bowl. Stir chocolate and walnuts into 1 portion; chopped cherries and red food coloring into second portion; and coconut and rum extract into third portion.

Line an 8-inch square baking dish with plastic wrap. Press chocolate mixture into dish. Top with rum mixture and cherry mixture, pressing gently. Cover and chill 8 hours.

Cut dough into 5 sections. Cut each section into ⅛-inch-thick slices. Arrange slices, 2 inches apart, on ungreased baking sheets.

Bake at 375° for 8 to 10 minutes or until lightly browned. Remove to wire racks to cool completely. Freeze up to 1 month, if desired. Yield: 8 dozen.

PECAN-BUTTER COOKIES
Prep: 18 minutes   Cook: 17 minutes per batch

*A hint of lemon comes through in these simple butter cookies.
They're good plain, and just plain good.*

1 cup butter, softened	½ teaspoon lemon extract
1 cup sugar	2 cups all-purpose flour
2 egg yolks	1 teaspoon baking powder
¾ teaspoon vanilla extract	¼ teaspoon salt
¾ teaspoon almond extract	¾ cup pecan halves

Beat butter at medium speed with an electric mixer until creamy; gradually add sugar, beating well. Add egg yolks, 1 at a time, and beat well after each addition. Stir in flavorings.

Combine flour, baking powder, and salt. Add to butter mixture, beating well.

Shape dough into 1-inch balls; place about 2 inches apart on ungreased baking sheets. Press a pecan half into center of each cookie.

Bake at 300° for 17 minutes or until edges are barely golden. Remove to wire racks to cool completely. Yield: 4 dozen.

DATE NUGGET COOKIES
Prep: 17 minutes   Cook: 12 minutes per batch

Chewy cookie lovers, stop here! These brown sugar and walnut wonders
trace their winning texture to chopped dates.

1 cup shortening
1¼ cups firmly packed brown sugar
3 large eggs
2½ cups all-purpose flour
1 teaspoon baking soda

½ teaspoon salt
1 tablespoon ground cinnamon
2 cups chopped walnuts
1½ cups chopped dates
1 teaspoon vanilla extract

Beat shortening at medium speed with an electric mixer until fluffy; gradually add sugar, beating well. Add eggs; beat well.

Combine flour and next 3 ingredients; gradually add to shortening mixture, beating well. Stir in walnuts, dates, and vanilla.

Shape dough into 1-inch balls; place 2 inches apart on greased baking sheets.

Bake at 350° for 12 minutes or until lightly browned. Cool slightly on baking sheets; remove to wire racks to cool completely. Yield: 3 dozen.

RUM BALLS

Prep: 18 minutes

Make these sugar-coated balls ahead—they get better each day.

1 (12-ounce) package vanilla wafers
1 (16-ounce) package pecan pieces
½ cup honey

⅓ cup bourbon
⅓ cup dark rum
⅓ cup powdered sugar

Process cookies in food processor until ground. Transfer to a large bowl. Process pecans in food processor until finely chopped. Stir into cookie crumbs. Stir in honey, bourbon, and rum. Shape dough into 1-inch balls, and roll in powdered sugar. Place in an airtight container; store in refrigerator up to 1 week. Yield: 6 dozen.

DOUBLE GINGER COOKIES

Prep: 18 minutes   Cook: 15 minutes per batch   Other: 1 hour

Small chunks of crystallized ginger add spark to these cookies, so chop it coarsely.
You can chill the dough for up to 24 hours before shaping and baking.

1½ cups all-purpose flour
1 cup whole wheat flour
¾ cup chopped crystallized ginger
1 teaspoon baking powder
½ teaspoon baking soda
½ teaspoon salt
½ teaspoon ground ginger

1¼ cups sugar, divided
½ cup applesauce
¼ cup vegetable oil
1 teaspoon grated lemon rind
1 tablespoon fresh lemon juice
¼ teaspoon vanilla extract

Combine first 7 ingredients; stir well with a whisk. Make a well in center of mixture. Combine 1 cup sugar, applesauce, and next 4 ingredients. Add to flour mixture, stirring just until moist; cover and chill dough at least 1 hour.

Lightly coat hands with flour (dough will be sticky). Shape dough into 24 balls (about 2 tablespoons each). Roll balls in ¼ cup sugar.

Place balls 2 inches apart on lightly greased baking sheets.

Bake at 350° for 15 minutes or until lightly browned. Cool 1 minute on baking sheets; remove to wire racks to cool completely. Yield: 2 dozen.

Note: These freeze well. Place cooled baked cookies in a zip-top freezer bag; freeze for up to 1 month. Thaw at room temperature.

EASY SANTA COOKIES

Prep: 40 minutes   Cook: 10 minutes per batch   Other· 1 hour

Kids and adults alike will have fun decorating these jolly St. Nick favorites.

1 cup butter or margarine,
    softened
½ cup granulated sugar
½ cup firmly packed brown sugar
1 large egg
3½ cups all-purpose flour
2 teaspoons baking powder
½ teaspoon salt
2 tablespoons milk
2 teaspoons vanilla extract

½ cup granulated sugar
2 (4¼-ounce) tubes red
    decorating frosting
2 (4¼-ounce) tubes white
    decorating frosting
½ cup semisweet chocolate morsels
    (3 ounces)
½ cup red cinnamon candies
1⅓ cups flaked coconut
60 miniature marshmallows

Beat butter at medium speed with an electric mixer until creamy; gradually add sugars, beating well. Add egg, beating well.

Combine flour, baking powder, and salt; add to butter mixture alternately with milk, beginning and ending with flour mixture. Mix at low speed after each addition until blended. Stir in vanilla.

Divide dough in half; wrap each half in plastic wrap. Chill 1 hour.

Shape dough into 1-inch balls, and place on lightly greased baking sheets. Dip a flat-bottomed glass into ½ cup sugar, and flatten balls to ¼-inch thickness.

Bake at 350° for 8 to 10 minutes or until golden. Remove to wire racks to cool completely.

Spread red frosting on top portion of cookie to resemble hat; spread white frosting on lower portion of cookie to resemble beard. Attach 2 chocolate morsels and 1 cinnamon candy with a small amount of frosting to resemble eyes and nose. Gently press coconut into white frosting. Press a marshmallow onto red frosting on each hat to resemble a tassel. Yield: 5 dozen.

HAZELNUT CRINKLE COOKIES

Prep: 18 minutes   Cook: 10 minutes per batch   Other: 10 minutes

This recipe bakes enough to share with friends—and keep for yourself.

½ cup chopped hazelnuts
1 (13-ounce) jar chocolate-
    hazelnut spread
¼ cup shortening
1⅓ cups granulated sugar
2 large eggs
1 teaspoon vanilla extract

3 cups all-purpose flour
2 teaspoons baking powder
½ teaspoon salt
⅓ cup milk
2 cups finely chopped hazelnuts
Sifted powdered sugar

Toast ½ cup chopped hazelnuts in a shallow pan at 350° for 5 to 10 minutes or until nuts smell fragrant. Set aside.

Beat chocolate-hazelnut spread and shortening at medium speed with an electric mixer until blended. Gradually add 1⅓ cups sugar, beating well. Add eggs and vanilla; beat until blended.

Combine flour, baking powder, and salt; add flour mixture to chocolate-hazelnut mixture alternately with milk, beginning and ending with flour mixture. Stir in toasted hazelnuts.

Shape dough into 1-inch balls; roll in finely chopped hazelnuts, and then in powdered sugar. Place 2 inches apart on lightly greased baking sheets.

Bake at 375° for 8 to 10 minutes or until set. Remove to wire racks to cool completely. Yield: 6 dozen.

CHERRY LEMON CROWNS

Prep: 25 minutes   Cook: 15 minutes per batch   Other: 2 hours

Cherries in the colors of Christmas dot these lemony butter cookies.

⅔ cup butter or margarine,
    softened
1 (3-ounce) package cream
   cheese, softened
1 cup sugar
1 egg yolk
1 teaspoon grated lemon rind
1 teaspoon fresh lemon juice
2 cups all-purpose flour
1 dozen each candied red and
   green cherries, halved
Lemon Glaze

Beat butter and cream cheese at medium speed with an electric mixer until creamy. Gradually add sugar, beating until light and fluffy. Add egg yolk, lemon rind, and lemon juice, beating well. Add flour, beating until blended. Cover and chill dough 2 hours.

Shape chilled dough into 1-inch balls. Place 2 inches apart on ungreased baking sheets. Flatten each ball into a 1½-inch disc. Press a candied cherry half into center of each cookie.

Bake at 350° for 12 to 15 minutes or until edges are barely golden. Cool 1 minute on baking sheets; remove to wire racks to cool completely. Drizzle lightly with Lemon Glaze. Let stand until glaze sets. Yield: 4 dozen.

Lemon Glaze:
Prep: 5 minutes

1½ cups sifted powdered sugar
1 to 2 tablespoons fresh lemon juice

Stir together powdered sugar and enough juice to make a good consistency. (Glaze should be thick, yet easy to drizzle.) Yield: enough for 4 dozen cookies.

CHOCOLATE-APRICOT THUMBPRINT COOKIES

Prep: 25 minutes   Cook: 18 minutes per batch   Other: 30 minutes

*Pockets of apricot preserves fill these pecan-coated cookies. A chocolate
drizzle dresses them up, but they're just as tempting unadorned.*

½ cup butter or margarine,
    softened
½ cup sugar
1 large egg, separated
1 teaspoon vanilla extract
1 cup all-purpose flour

¼ teaspoon salt
2 cups finely chopped pecans,
    divided
½ cup apricot preserves
½ cup semisweet chocolate
    morsels (3 ounces), melted

Beat butter at medium speed with an electric
mixer until creamy; gradually add sugar,
beating until fluffy. Add egg yolk and vanilla; beat well.

Combine flour and salt; add to butter
mixture, beating well. Stir in 1 cup pecans.
Cover and chill dough at least 30 minutes.

Lightly beat egg white. Shape dough
into 1-inch balls; dip each ball in egg white,
and roll in remaining 1 cup pecans. Place
balls 1 inch apart on greased baking sheets.
Press thumb gently into center of each ball
to make an indentation; fill with preserves.

Bake at 350° for 17 to 18 minutes or
until lightly browned. Cool 1 minute on
baking sheets; remove to wire racks to cool
completely.

Drizzle melted chocolate over cooled
cookies, using a fork or spoon. Yield:
3 dozen.

CHOCOLATE SNOWBALLS

Prep: 25 minutes   Cook: 10 minutes per batch

Young would-be chefs will delight in rolling these balls in powdered sugar.

1¼ cups butter, softened
⅔ cup granulated sugar
2 teaspoons vanilla extract
2 cups all-purpose flour
½ cup unsweetened cocoa

¼ teaspoon salt
½ cup finely chopped unsalted
      peanuts
Sifted powdered sugar

Beat butter at medium speed with an electric mixer until creamy; gradually add granulated sugar and vanilla, beating well. Combine flour, cocoa, salt, and nuts; gradually add to butter mixture, beating until blended.

Shape dough into 1-inch balls; place on ungreased baking sheets.

Bake at 350° for 8 to 10 minutes. Roll warm cookies in powdered sugar. Yield: about 7 dozen.

SPICED MADELEINES

Prep: 20 minutes   Cook: 9 minutes per batch

These delicate cookies take their name from the ribbed cookie mold they're baked in.
Be sure to grease every crevice of the molds so the cookies will pop out easily.

4 large eggs
¼ teaspoon salt
⅔ cup granulated sugar
1 cup all-purpose flour
1 teaspoon ground cinnamon

½ teaspoon ground nutmeg
¼ teaspoon ground cloves
½ cup butter or margarine, melted
Powdered sugar

Beat eggs and salt at medium speed with an electric mixer until foamy (about 2 minutes). Gradually add granulated sugar; beat at high speed 15 minutes or until thickened.

Combine flour and next 3 ingredients; stir into egg mixture. Fold in butter, 1 tablespoon at a time. Spoon about 1 tablespoon batter into each lightly greased madeleine mold.

Bake at 400° for 7 to 9 minutes or until lightly browned. Carefully remove from molds to wire racks to cool completely, flat side down. Sprinkle with powdered sugar. Yield: 2½ dozen.

CHERRY ICEBOX COOKIES

Prep: 13 minutes   Cook: 10 minutes per batch   Other: 2 hours

Maraschino cherries and red decorator sugar dress these icebox cookies for Christmas.

1 cup butter, softened
1 cup granulated sugar
1 large egg
1 teaspoon vanilla extract
2¾ cups all-purpose flour
1 teaspoon baking powder
½ teaspoon salt

1 (16-ounce) jar maraschino
    cherries, drained and finely
    chopped
1 cup finely chopped pecans
¼ cup red decorator sugar
    crystals (optional)

Beat butter at medium speed with an electric mixer until creamy; gradually add 1 cup sugar, beating well. Add egg and vanilla, beating well.

Combine flour, baking powder, and salt; add to butter mixture, beating well. Pat cherries between paper towels to remove excess moisture. Stir cherries and pecans into dough; cover and chill at least 2 hours.

Shape dough into 2 (8-inch) rolls. Roll in sugar crystals, if desired. Wrap rolls in wax paper, and chill or freeze until firm.

Slice chilled dough into ¼-inch slices, using a sharp knife. Place on lightly greased baking sheets.

Bake at 400° for 8 to 10 minutes or until golden. Cool 1 minute on baking sheets; remove to wire racks to cool completely. Yield: 4 dozen.

Note: If desired, substitute green candied cherries for maraschino cherries, and roll the logs of dough in green decorator sugar crystals.

LEMON ICEBOX COOKIES

Prep: 20 minutes   Cook: 14 minutes per batch   Other: 8 hours

You can freeze this simple dough up to two months.

1 cup butter, softened
1 cup granulated sugar
1 cup firmly packed light brown
   sugar
2 large eggs

1 teaspoon grated lemon rind
2 tablespoons fresh lemon juice
3½ cups all-purpose flour
1 teaspoon baking soda
½ teaspoon salt

Beat butter and sugars at medium speed with an electric mixer until fluffy. Add eggs, 1 at a time, beating well after each addition. Add grated lemon rind and lemon juice, beating until blended.

Combine flour, baking soda, and salt; gradually add to butter mixture, beating just until blended. Divide dough into 3 equal portions; roll each portion on wax paper into a 12-inch log. Cover and chill 8 hours.

Slice chilled dough into ½-inch slices, and place on lightly greased baking sheets.

Bake at 350° for 12 to 14 minutes or until edges are lightly browned. Remove to wire racks to cool completely. Store in an airtight container; freeze, if desired. Yield: 7 dozen.

Lemon-Coconut Cookies: Stir 1 cup toasted coconut into dough; proceed with recipe as directed.

Lemon-Almond Cookies: Stir 1 cup sliced almonds, toasted, into dough; proceed with recipe as directed.

Lemon-Poppy Seed Cookies: Stir 2 teaspoons poppy seeds into dough; proceed with recipe as directed.

Lemon-Pecan Cookies: Stir 1 cup finely chopped pecans, toasted, into dough; proceed with recipe as directed.

CRANBERRY-WALNUT SWIRLS

Prep: 15 minutes   Cook: 15 minutes per batch   Other: 9 hours

*These cookies make such a pretty presentation, you'll want
to package them in clear containers.*

½ cup butter or margarine, softened
¾ cup sugar
1 large egg
1 teaspoon vanilla extract
1½ cups all-purpose flour
¼ teaspoon baking powder

¼ teaspoon salt
⅓ cup finely chopped fresh
    cranberries
½ cup ground walnuts
1 tablespoon grated orange rind

Beat butter and sugar at medium speed with an electric mixer until light and fluffy. Add egg and vanilla, beating until blended. Gradually add flour, baking powder, and salt, beating until blended. Cover and chill 1 hour.

Combine cranberries, walnuts, and orange rind.

Turn dough out onto a lightly floured surface, and roll into a 10-inch square.

Sprinkle with cranberry mixture, leaving a ½-inch border on 2 opposite sides.

Roll up dough, jellyroll fashion, beginning at a bordered side. Cover and freeze 8 hours or up to 1 month. Cut roll into ¼-inch-thick slices. Place slices on lightly greased baking sheets.

Bake on top oven rack at 375° for 14 to 15 minutes or until lightly browned. Remove to wire racks to cool completely. Yield: 3 dozen.

SLICE-AND-BAKE OATMEAL COOKIES

Prep: 18 minutes   Cook: 10 minutes per batch   Other: 6 hours

Keep this dough in your freezer for a quick home-baked treat anytime.

1½ cups all-purpose flour
1 teaspoon baking soda
½ teaspoon salt
1 cup shortening
1 cup granulated sugar

1 cup firmly packed brown sugar
2 eggs
1 teaspoon vanilla extract
3 cups uncooked quick-cooking oats
½ cup chopped pecans

Combine flour, soda, and salt; stir well, and set aside.

Beat shortening; gradually add sugars, beating well at medium speed with an electric mixer; add eggs and vanilla, beating well. Add flour mixture, beating well. Stir in oats and pecans. Shape dough into 2 (12-inch) rolls; wrap in wax paper, and chill at least 6 hours.

Unwrap rolls, and cut into ¼-inch slices; place on ungreased baking sheets.

Bake at 375° for 8 to 10 minutes or until lightly browned. Remove to wire racks to cool completely. Yield: about 7 dozen.

Note: Dough can be frozen up to 3 months. Slice dough while frozen, and bake at 375° for 12 minutes.

VANILLA SLICE-AND-BAKE COOKIES

Prep: 18 minutes   Cook: 12 minutes per batch   Other: 2 hours

You can welcome drop-in guests with a tasty treat, warm from the oven,
if you keep a log of this dough on hand in the freezer.

½ cup butter or margarine,
    softened
1 cup sugar
1 egg
2 teaspoons vanilla extract

1¾ cups all-purpose flour
½ teaspoon baking soda
¼ teaspoon salt
½ cup chopped pecans

Beat butter at medium speed with an electric mixer; gradually add sugar, beating well. Add egg and vanilla; beat well. Combine flour, soda, and salt; add to butter mixture, beating well. Stir in pecans. Shape dough into 2 (12-inch) rolls; wrap in wax paper, and chill at least 2 hours.

Unwrap rolls, and cut into ¼-inch slices; place on ungreased baking sheets.

Bake at 350° for 10 to 12 minutes. Cool slightly on baking sheets; remove to wire racks to cool completely. Yield: 7 dozen.

Slice of Spice Cookies: Prepare Vanilla Slice-and-Bake Cookies, substituting firmly packed brown sugar for granulated sugar. Combine ¼ cup granulated sugar and 2 teaspoons ground cinnamon; dip each cookie slice (on both sides) in mixture before baking.

Note: Dough can be frozen up to 3 months. Slice dough while frozen, and bake as directed.

PEPPERMINT PATTIES

Prep: 35 minutes   Cook: 11 minutes per batch   Other: 5 hours

*Coarsely crush the peppermint candies to adorn these ice cream sandwich cookies
in a large zip-top freezer bag by lightly tapping them with a rolling pin
or heavy skillet (a food processor pulverizes them).*

1½ cups all-purpose flour
⅓ cup Dutch process cocoa or
    regular unsweetened cocoa
½ teaspoon baking soda
¼ teaspoon salt
½ cup butter, softened
½ cup granulated sugar

½ cup firmly packed brown sugar
1 large egg
1 teaspoon vanilla extract
30 hard peppermint candies,
    crushed (about 1 cup)
4 cups vanilla ice cream, softened

Stir together first 4 ingredients in a bowl; set aside.

Beat butter and sugars at medium speed with an electric mixer until blended. Add egg and vanilla; beat until blended. Gradually add flour mixture to sugar mixture; beat at low speed just until blended.

Lightly grease hands with cooking spray. Divide dough in half. Shape each half into a 6-inch log. Wrap logs individually in plastic wrap; freeze 1 hour or until firm.

Working with 1 log at a time, cut each log into 12 (½-inch) slices; place cookies 1 inch apart on lightly greased baking sheets.

Bake at 350° for 11 minutes or until set. Let stand 2 minutes on baking sheets. Remove to wire racks to cool completely.

Place crushed candies on a shallow plate. Carefully spread ⅓ cup ice cream onto bottom sides of each of 12 cookies. Top with remaining cookies, bottom sides down, pressing gently. Quickly roll the sides of each sandwich in candy. Wrap each sandwich tightly in plastic wrap; freeze 4 hours or until firm. Yield: 1 dozen.

PFEFFERNÜESSE

Prep: 26 minutes   Cook: 10 minutes per batch   Other: 3 hours

A German favorite at Christmastime, these "peppernut" cookies are flavored with sweet spices and black pepper, which give them an unusual kick.

¾ cup butter or margarine, softened

1 cup granulated sugar

1 cup dark corn syrup

3 tablespoons hot water

2 teaspoons anise seed

1 teaspoon black pepper

1 teaspoon baking soda

¼ teaspoon salt

¼ teaspoon ground allspice

¼ teaspoon ground cardamom

¼ teaspoon ground cloves

4 to 4½ cups all-purpose flour, divided

1 cup sifted powdered sugar

Beat butter at medium speed with an electric mixer until creamy; gradually add granulated sugar, beating well. Add corn syrup and next 8 ingredients; beat at low speed until blended.

Gradually add 4 cups flour to butter mixture, beating at low speed until blended after each addition. Stir in enough remaining flour to form a stiff dough. Cover and chill 3 hours.

Divide dough into 8 equal portions; roll each portion into a ½-inch-thick rope. Cut ropes into 1-inch lengths, and place 2 inches apart on ungreased baking sheets.

Bake at 350° for 10 minutes or until golden brown. Remove to wire racks to cool completely. Roll cooled cookies in powdered sugar. Yield: 5 dozen.

MELT-AWAY BUTTER COOKIES

Prep: 20 minutes   Cook: 15 minutes per batch

Melt-away Butter Cookies call for a cookie press, which you can use to quickly stamp out a wide variety of perfectly shaped cookies. A cookie press is a practical investment for someone who does a lot of baking and entertaining.

1¼ cups butter, softened
¾ cup sifted powdered sugar
2½ cups all-purpose flour
½ teaspoon vanilla extract

½ teaspoon almond extract
Few drops of liquid food
      coloring (optional)

Beat butter at medium speed with an electric mixer until creamy; gradually add sugar, beating well. Add flour, and mix well. Stir in flavorings and, if desired, food coloring.

Use a cookie press to shape dough as desired, following manufacturer's instructions. Place cookies on ungreased baking sheets.

Bake at 325° for 15 minutes. Remove to wire racks to cool completely. Store cookies in airtight containers, placing wax paper between each layer. Yield: about 7 dozen (2-inch) cookies.

Chocolate-Tipped Butter Cookies: Melt 1 (12-ounce) package semisweet chocolate morsels (2 cups) and 1 tablespoon shortening. Dip half of each baked cookie into chocolate mixture. Roll chocolate-dipped portion in ½ cup finely chopped pecans. Place cookies on wire racks until chocolate is firm.

BLACK-EYED SUSANS

Prep: 20 minutes   Cook: 8 minutes per batch

A chocolate morsel adorns the center of each flower-shaped cookie.

½ cup butter or margarine,
    softened
½ cup granulated sugar
½ cup firmly packed brown sugar
1 cup creamy peanut butter
1 large egg
1½ tablespoons warm water

1 teaspoon vanilla extract
1½ cups all-purpose flour
½ teaspoon baking soda
½ teaspoon salt
½ to 1 cup semisweet chocolate
    morsels (3 ounces to 6 ounces)

Beat butter and sugars at medium speed with an electric mixer until light and fluffy. Add peanut butter and next 3 ingredients, beating well. Combine flour, baking soda, and salt. Add to butter mixture, beating until blended.

Use a cookie press fitted with a flower-shaped disc to shape dough into cookies, following manufacturer's instructions. Press cookies onto lightly greased baking sheets. Place a chocolate morsel in center of each cookie.

Bake at 350° for 8 minutes or until lightly browned. Remove to wire racks to cool completely. Yield: 8 dozen.

Heavenly Chocolate
Chunk Cookies
(page 82)

chapter

3

drop
cookies

HEAVENLY CHOCOLATE CHUNK COOKIES

Prep: 20 minutes   Cook: 14 minutes per batch

Discover a big chocolate taste in every bite of these deluxe chocolate chip cookies (pictured on page 80).

¾ cup butter or margarine

2 tablespoons instant coffee
    granules

2 cups plus 2 tablespoons
    all-purpose flour

½ teaspoon baking soda

½ teaspoon salt

1 cup firmly packed brown sugar

½ cup granulated sugar

1 large egg

1 egg yolk

1 (11.5-ounce) package semisweet
    chocolate chunks

1 cup walnut halves, toasted

Combine butter and coffee granules in a saucepan or skillet. Cook over medium-low heat until butter melts and coffee granules dissolve, stirring occasionally. Remove from heat, and let mixture cool to room temperature (don't let butter resolidify).

Combine flour, soda, and salt; stir well.

Combine butter mixture, sugars, egg, and egg yolk in a large bowl. Beat at medium speed with an electric mixer until blended.

Gradually add flour mixture, beating at low speed just until blended. Stir in chocolate chunks and walnuts.

Drop dough by heaping tablespoonfuls 2 inches apart onto ungreased baking sheets.

Bake at 325° for 12 to 14 minutes. Let cool slightly on baking sheets. Remove to wire racks to cool completely. Yield: 20 cookies.

WHITE CHOCOLATE DREAM COOKIES

Prep: 15 minutes   Cook: 12 minutes per batch

You'll have to pinch yourself after you taste these luscious white
chocolate chip cookies laced with a heavenly hint of orange.

1 cup butter, softened

⅔ cup firmly packed light brown
    sugar

½ cup granulated sugar

1 large egg

1 tablespoon grated orange rind

2 teaspoons orange extract

2¼ cups all-purpose flour

¾ teaspoon baking soda

½ teaspoon salt

1 (12-ounce) package white
    chocolate morsels (2 cups)

Beat first 3 ingredients at medium speed with an electric mixer until creamy. Add egg, orange rind, and extract, beating until blended.

Combine flour, baking soda, and salt; gradually add to sugar mixture, beating just until blended. Stir in morsels.

Drop dough by rounded tablespoonfuls onto ungreased baking sheets.

Bake at 350° for 10 to 12 minutes or until edges of cookies are lightly browned. Cool on baking sheets 2 minutes. Remove to wire racks to cool completely. Yield: 3½ dozen.

MOLASSES OATMEAL COOKIES

Prep: 10 minutes   Cook: 10 minutes per batch

Sweeten traditional oatmeal cookies with the rich flavor of molasses.

½ cup shortening
1½ cups sugar
½ cup molasses
2 large eggs
1¾ cups all-purpose flour
1 teaspoon baking soda

1 teaspoon salt
1 teaspoon ground cinnamon
2 cups uncooked regular oats
1½ cups raisins
¾ cup chopped pecans

Beat first 3 ingredients at medium speed with an electric mixer until blended. Add eggs, beating until blended.

Combine flour and next 3 ingredients. Add to shortening mixture, beating until blended. Stir in oats, raisins, and pecans.

Drop dough by heaping teaspoonfuls 2 inches apart onto lightly greased baking sheets.

Bake at 350° for 10 minutes or until golden; remove to wire racks to cool completely. Yield: 7 dozen.

OATMEAL-BUTTERSCOTCH CHIPPERS

Prep: 12 minutes   Cook: 11 minutes per batch

Oats take the place of flour in these crispy-edged butterscotch cookies.

1¼ cups butter-flavored shortening

1¼ cups extra-crunchy peanut
     butter

1½ cups firmly packed brown sugar

1 cup granulated sugar

3 large eggs

4½ cups uncooked regular oats

2 teaspoons baking powder

1½ cups butterscotch morsels
    (9 ounces)

1 (6-ounce) package semisweet
    chocolate morsels (1 cup)

1 cup chopped pecans or pecan
    pieces

Beat shortening and peanut butter at medium speed with an electric mixer until creamy; gradually add sugars, beating well. Add eggs, 1 at a time, beating until blended after each addition.

Combine oats and baking powder; add to shortening mixture, beating well. Stir in morsels and pecans.

Drop dough by rounded teaspoonfuls onto ungreased baking sheets.

Bake at 350° for 9 to 11 minutes or until lightly browned. Cool 2 minutes on baking sheets; remove to wire racks to cool completely. Yield: 7 dozen.

Jumbo Oatmeal-Butterscotch Chippers: Drop dough by 2 tablespoonfuls 2 inches apart onto ungreased baking sheets. Bake at 350° for 11 to 12 minutes or until lightly browned. Yield: 4½ dozen.

SANTA'S BACKPACK COOKIES
Prep: 12 minutes   Cook: 12 minutes per batch

Peanuts, cereal, and chocolate candy pieces are packed into these goodies.

1 cup butter or margarine,
   softened
1 cup granulated sugar
1 cup firmly packed brown sugar
2 large eggs
1 teaspoon vanilla extract
2 cups all-purpose flour
1 teaspoon baking soda
½ teaspoon baking powder
⅛ teaspoon salt

1 cup uncooked regular oats
2 cups crisp rice cereal
2 cups candy-coated chocolate
   pieces
1 cup chopped unsalted roasted
   peanuts
½ cup flaked coconut
1 (6-ounce) package semisweet
   chocolate morsels (1 cup)

Beat butter at medium speed with an electric mixer until creamy; gradually add sugars, beating well. Add eggs and vanilla; beat well.

Combine flour and next 3 ingredients; gradually add to butter mixture, mixing well. Stir in oats and remaining ingredients.

Drop dough by rounded tablespoonfuls 2 inches apart onto ungreased baking sheets.

Bake at 350° for 10 to 12 minutes or until cookies are lightly browned; remove to wire racks to cool completely. Yield: 6 dozen.

OATMEAL-NUT-CHOCOLATE CHIP COOKIES

Prep: 22 minutes   Cook: 12 minutes per batch

Dipping these classic cookies in melted chocolate makes them a chocolate lover's dream.

1½ cups uncooked regular oats
1 cup butter or margarine, softened
1 cup granulated sugar
1 cup firmly packed brown sugar
2 large eggs
1 tablespoon vanilla extract
2 cups all-purpose flour
1 teaspoon baking soda
½ teaspoon baking powder

½ teaspoon salt
1 (12-ounce) package semisweet
    chocolate morsels (2 cups)
3 (1.5-ounce) bars milk chocolate,
    grated
1½ cups chopped pecans
6 (2-ounce) chocolate bark coating
    squares, melted (optional)

Place oats in an electric blender; process until finely ground. Set aside.

Beat butter in a large bowl at medium speed with an electric mixer until creamy; gradually add sugars, beating well. Add eggs and vanilla; beat well.

Combine ground oats, flour, and next 3 ingredients; gradually add flour mixture to butter mixture, mixing well. Stir in chocolate morsels, grated chocolate, and pecans.

Drop dough by heaping teaspoonfuls onto greased baking sheets.

Bake at 375° for 10 to 12 minutes or until lightly browned. Let cool slightly; remove to wire racks to cool completely.

Dip half of each cookie in melted bark coating, if desired; place on wax paper to dry. Yield: about 9 dozen.

ORANGE SLICE COOKIES

Prep: 12 minutes   Cook: 10 minutes per batch

These chewy spice cookies turn out nine dozen golden gems—perfect for packing lots of gift packages.

1½ cups chopped candy orange
        slices
¼ cup all-purpose flour
1 cup butter or margarine,
        softened
1 cup firmly packed brown
        sugar
¾ cup granulated sugar
2 large eggs
2 tablespoons milk

2 teaspoons vanilla extract
2 cups all-purpose flour
1 teaspoon baking soda
½ teaspoon salt
½ teaspoon ground cinnamon
½ teaspoon ground nutmeg
2½ cups uncooked quick-cooking
        oats
1 cup flaked coconut

Combine chopped orange slices and ¼ cup flour in a medium bowl, tossing to coat candy; set aside. Beat butter at medium speed with an electric mixer until creamy; gradually add sugars, beating well. Add eggs, milk, and vanilla; beat well.

Combine 2 cups flour and next 4 ingredients; gradually add to butter mixture, beating well. Stir in candy mixture, oats, and coconut.

Drop dough by rounded teaspoonfuls 2 inches apart onto greased baking sheets.

Bake at 375° for 10 minutes or until lightly browned. Cool slightly on baking sheets; remove to wire racks to cool completely. Yield: 9 dozen.

CRISPY PRALINE COOKIES
Prep: 10 minutes   Cook: 15 minutes per batch

All the flavors of the traditional candy highlight these crispy cookies.

1 cup all-purpose flour
1 cup firmly packed dark brown
    sugar
1 large egg
1 cup chopped pecans
½ cup butter, softened
1 teaspoon vanilla extract

Stir together all ingredients in a large bowl, blending well. Drop cookie dough by table-spoonfuls onto ungreased baking sheets.

Bake at 350° for 13 to 15 minutes. Cool on baking sheets 1 minute; remove cookies to wire racks to cool completely. Yield: about 2 dozen.

Crispy Praline-Chocolate Chip Cookies: Add 1 cup semisweet chocolate morsels; bake as directed.

CRANBERRY-ALMOND COOKIES

Prep: 20 minutes   Cook: 11 minutes per batch

*Take advantage of this plentiful winter fruit to whip up a
few batches of this chewy Christmas treat.*

1 cup butter, softened
¾ cup granulated sugar
¾ cup firmly packed light brown
    sugar
½ teaspoon almond extract
2 large eggs

2¼ cups all-purpose flour
1 teaspoon baking powder
1 teaspoon salt
2 cups chopped fresh cranberries
1 cup slivered almonds, toasted

Beat butter at medium speed with an electric mixer until creamy; gradually add sugars, beating well. Add extract and eggs, beating until blended.

Combine flour, baking powder, and salt in a small bowl; gradually add to butter mixture, beating at low speed until blended after each addition. Stir cranberries and almonds into batter.

Drop dough by rounded tablespoonfuls 2 inches apart onto ungreased baking sheets.

Bake at 375° for 9 to 11 minutes. Remove to wire racks to cool completely. Yield: 3½ dozen.

BUTTERCRISP COOKIES

Prep: 17 minutes   Cook: 9 minutes per batch   Other: 30 minutes

These crispy-edged cookies have bits of candy in every bite. Baking them on parchment paper makes it easier to transfer them to wire racks.

¾ cup unsalted butter, softened
¾ cup granulated sugar
¾ cup firmly packed brown
     sugar
2 large eggs
2¼ cups all-purpose flour
2 teaspoons baking powder
1 teaspoon salt

1 tablespoon vanilla extract
1 (6-ounce) package white
     chocolate baking squares,
     coarsely chopped
6 (2.1-ounce) chocolate-covered
     crispy peanut-buttery candy
     bars, coarsely chopped
1 cup uncooked regular oats

Beat butter at medium speed with an electric mixer until creamy. Add sugars, beating until fluffy. Add eggs, 1 at a time, beating just until blended.

Combine flour, baking powder, and salt. Gradually add flour mixture to butter mixture, beating until blended. Stir in vanilla. Stir in white chocolate, candy, and oats.

Cover and chill dough 30 minutes.

Drop dough by heaping teaspoonfuls 2 inches apart onto parchment paper-lined baking sheets.

Bake at 350° for 8 to 9 minutes or until golden (do not overbake). Cool 5 minutes on baking sheets; remove to wire racks to cool completely. Yield: 5 dozen.

PEANUT BUTTER-TOFFEE TURTLE COOKIES

Prep: 25 minutes   Cook: 12 minutes per batch

The chocolate drizzle on the cookies will harden as it cools.

⅔ cup creamy peanut butter
½ cup unsalted butter, softened
½ cup granulated sugar
½ cup firmly packed light brown
    sugar
1 large egg
2 cups all-purpose baking mix
⅔ cup toffee bits

⅔ cup coarsely chopped peanuts
⅔ cup milk chocolate morsels
10 ounces vanilla caramels
2 to 3 tablespoons whipping
    cream
½ teaspoon vanilla extract
⅔ cup milk chocolate morsels, melted

Beat first 4 ingredients at medium speed with an electric mixer until creamy. Add egg, beating until blended. Add baking mix, beating at low speed just until blended. Stir in toffee bits, chopped peanuts, and ⅔ cup chocolate morsels.

Drop dough by rounded tablespoonfuls onto ungreased baking sheets; flatten dough with hand.

Bake at 350° for 10 to 12 minutes or until golden brown. Cool on baking sheets

1 minute; remove to wire racks to cool completely.

Microwave caramels and 2 tablespoons whipping cream in a glass bowl at HIGH 1 minute; stir. Continue to microwave at 30-second intervals, stirring until caramels melt and mixture is smooth; add remaining cream, if necessary. Stir in vanilla. Spoon caramel mixture evenly onto tops of cookies; drizzle evenly with melted chocolate. Yield: 3 dozen.

MIXED NUT TURTLES

Prep: 15 minutes   Cook: 12 minutes per batch

Melted chocolate nestles between salty nuts on this candylike cookie.

¾ cup butter, softened
½ cup sugar
1 egg yolk
1 teaspoon vanilla extract
1½ cups all-purpose flour
1 (9.75-ounce) can mixed nuts
    (almonds, macadamia nuts,
    and cashews)

1½ cups semisweet chocolate
    morsels (9 ounces)
2 teaspoons shortening

Beat butter at medium speed with an electric mixer until creamy. Gradually add sugar, beating well. Add egg yolk and vanilla, beating well. Add flour to butter mixture, beating just until blended.

Drop dough by level tablespoonfuls 2 inches apart onto ungreased baking sheets. Flatten each ball of dough into a 2-inch circle, using fingers.

Cut large macadamia nuts in half. Press nuts firmly into outside top edges of cookies.

Bake at 350° for 10 to 12 minutes or until edges are lightly browned. Cool 1 minute on baking sheets. Carefully remove cookies to wire racks to cool completely.

Heat chocolate and shortening in a heavy saucepan over low heat, stirring until melted.

Spoon 1 heaping teaspoon melted chocolate onto center of each cookie. Spread and smooth chocolate between nuts. Let set until chocolate hardens. Yield: 2 dozen.

COFFEE BEAN COOKIES

Prep: 25 minutes   Cook: 11 minutes per batch

These rich drop cookies are studded with chocolate-covered coffee beans,
chunks of toffee candy bars, and almonds.

½ cup butter, softened
½ cup shortening
¾ cup granulated sugar
¾ cup firmly packed brown sugar
2 large eggs
1 teaspoon vanilla extract
2¼ cups all-purpose flour
1 teaspoon baking soda

1 teaspoon salt
½ teaspoon ground cinnamon
1 cup chopped almonds, toasted
3 (2-ounce) packages chocolate-
    covered coffee beans (1 cup)
4 (1.4-ounce) English toffee
    candy bars, chopped (about
    1 cup)

Beat butter and shortening at medium speed with an electric mixer until creamy; gradually add sugars, beating well. Add eggs and vanilla; beat well.

Combine flour and next 3 ingredients; add to butter mixture, beating well.

Stir in chopped almonds, chocolate-covered coffee beans, and chopped English toffee candy bars. Cover and chill dough, if desired.

Drop dough by heaping teaspoonfuls onto ungreased baking sheets.

Bake at 350° for 10 to 11 minutes or until golden. Cool 1 minute on baking sheets; remove to wire racks to cool completely. Yield: 4 dozen.

OLD-FASHIONED FRUITCAKE COOKIES

Prep: 17 minutes   Cook: 12 minutes per batch

Bake up a twist on a classic Christmas cake with these chewy favorites.

2 cups chopped pecans
½ pound candied pineapple,
    chopped
½ pound red and green candied
    cherries, chopped
½ pound golden raisins
¼ cup all-purpose flour

½ cup butter or margarine,
    softened
1 cup firmly packed brown sugar
4 large eggs
2½ cups all-purpose flour
1 teaspoon baking soda
¾ teaspoon ground cardamom

Combine first 5 ingredients in a large bowl, tossing to coat fruit and nuts with flour.

Beat butter at medium speed with an electric mixer until creamy; gradually add brown sugar, beating well. Add eggs, and beat well.

Combine 2½ cups flour, baking soda, and cardamom in a bowl; gradually add to butter mixture, beating well. Stir in fruit mixture.

Drop dough by heaping teaspoonfuls 2 inches apart onto lightly greased baking sheets.

Bake at 350° for 12 minutes or until lightly browned. Cool slightly on baking sheets; remove to wire racks to cool completely. Yield: 9½ dozen.

EASY CAKE MIX COOKIES

Prep: 5 minutes   Cook: 10 minutes per batch

What could be simpler than a cookie that begins with a cake mix?

1 (18.25-ounce) package
    chocolate or yellow cake mix
½ cup vegetable oil
2 large eggs

1 (6-ounce) package semisweet
    chocolate morsels (1 cup)
½ cup chopped pecans

Beat first 3 ingredients at medium speed with an electric mixer until smooth. Stir in chocolate and pecans. Drop by heaping teaspoonfuls onto ungreased baking sheets.

Bake at 350° for 8 to 10 minutes. Let cool 1 minute on baking sheet; remove to wire racks to cool completely. Yield: 4½ dozen.

Holiday Candy
Fudge Bars
(page 104)

bar
cookies

HOLIDAY CANDY FUDGE BARS

Prep: 18 minutes   Cook: 38 minutes

The red and green candies that dot this rich bar (pictured on page 102)
add a festive touch to this holiday dessert—that is, while it lasts!

2 cups uncooked quick-cooking
    oats
1½ cups all-purpose flour
1 cup chopped pecans
1 cup firmly packed light brown
    sugar
1 teaspoon baking soda

¼ teaspoon salt
1 cup butter or margarine, melted
1½ cups red and green candy-
    coated chocolate pieces,
    divided
1 (14-ounce) can sweetened
    condensed milk

Combine first 6 ingredients, stirring well. Add butter, and stir or beat at low speed with an electric mixer until mixture is crumbly. Reserve 1½ cups crumb mixture; press remaining crumb mixture into a lightly greased 13- x 9-inch pan. Bake at 375° for 10 minutes. Cool on a wire rack. Reduce oven temperature to 350°.

Place 1 cup chocolate pieces in a microwave-safe bowl; microwave at HIGH 1 to 1½ minutes, stirring after 30 seconds. Press chocolate pieces with the back of a spoon to mash them. (The candies will almost be melted with pieces of color coating still visible.) Stir in condensed milk. Spread mixture evenly over crust in pan, leaving a ½-inch border on all sides.

Combine reserved 1½ cups crumb mixture and remaining ½ cup chocolate pieces; sprinkle evenly over chocolate mixture, and press lightly.

Bake at 350° for 25 to 28 minutes or until golden. Cool in pan on a wire rack. Cut into bars. Yield: 3 dozen.

CONGO BARS

Prep: 10 minutes   Cook: 27 minutes

We're not sure how this dessert got its name, but we do know it's similar to a blond brownie, and it's loaded with chunky chocolate chips and nuts. The cookies are popular in the South.

½ cup butter or margarine, melted

2 cups firmly packed brown sugar

3 large eggs, lightly beaten

1 teaspoon vanilla extract

1½ cups all-purpose flour

1 cup chocolate graham cracker crumbs (about 6 whole crackers)

2 teaspoons baking powder

1 cup salted cashews, chopped

1 (11.5-ounce) package semisweet chocolate chunks

Stir together first 4 ingredients. Combine flour, graham cracker crumbs, and baking powder; add to butter mixture, stirring well. Stir in cashews and chocolate chunks. (Batter will be thick.)

Spoon batter into a lightly greased 13- x 9-inch pan; press gently into pan.

Bake at 350° for 27 minutes. Cool completely in pan on a wire rack. Cut into bars, using a sharp knife. Yield: 2 dozen.

WHITE CHOCOLATE-ALMOND BLONDIES

Prep: 10 minutes   Cook: 30 minutes

These chewy blonde brownies are full of almonds and buttery white chocolate bits.

2 cups all-purpose flour

1½ teaspoons baking powder

½ teaspoon salt

⅔ cup butter or margarine

1½ teaspoons instant coffee
    granules

2 cups firmly packed brown sugar

2 large eggs, lightly beaten

1 cup whole natural almonds,
    coarsely chopped and toasted

1 (6-ounce) package white
    chocolate morsels (1 cup)

Combine flour, baking powder, and salt in a bowl; set aside.

Melt butter in a large saucepan over medium-low heat. Add coffee granules, stirring until dissolved. Remove from heat. Add brown sugar and eggs; stir well. Gradually stir in flour mixture. Add almonds and white chocolate morsels, stirring well.

Spread batter in a lightly greased 13- x 9-inch pan. Bake at 350° for 30 minutes. Cool in pan on a wire rack. Cut into squares. Yield: 2½ dozen.

LEMON-COCONUT BAR COOKIES

Prep: 22 minutes   Cook: 32 minutes

Slip these tart cookies into a box lined with wax paper. Or keep them in the pan and make that part of your gift.

1   cup all-purpose flour
2   tablespoons granulated sugar
¼   cup chilled butter, cut into small
    pieces
1   cup firmly packed brown sugar
3   tablespoons fresh lemon juice

2   large eggs
½   cup sweetened flaked coconut
⅔   cup powdered sugar
1   teaspoon grated lemon rind
2   tablespoons fresh lemon juice

Combine flour and granulated sugar in a bowl; cut in butter with a pastry blender or 2 knives until mixture resembles coarse meal.

Press mixture into a lightly greased 9-inch square pan. Bake at 350° for 10 minutes.

Combine brown sugar, 3 tablespoons lemon juice, and eggs in a medium bowl, stirring with a whisk. Stir in coconut; pour evenly into pan. Bake 22 more minutes or until set.

Whisk together powdered sugar, rind, and 2 tablespoons juice. Spread glaze evenly over cookies. Cool completely in pan on a wire rack. Cut into bars. Yield: 1½ dozen.

COCONUT-RASPBERRY LINZER BARS

Prep: 15 minutes   Cook: 38 minutes

Reminiscent of the Austrian linzertorte, these pretty bars flaunt a shortbread crust flavored with lemon zest, cinnamon, and ground almonds that's spread with jam and topped with a pastry lattice design.

1½ cups all-purpose flour
1 cup slivered almonds
½ cup sweetened flaked coconut
¼ cup sugar
½ teaspoon ground cinnamon
½ teaspoon grated lemon rind
¼ teaspoon salt
¼ teaspoon ground cloves
¾ cup cold butter, cut into pieces
2 egg yolks
1 cup seedless raspberry jam
Garnish: powdered sugar

Process first 8 ingredients in a food processor until almonds are finely ground. Add butter; pulse 10 times or until crumbly. Add egg yolks; process 15 seconds or until dough forms a ball. Set aside one-third of dough. Press remaining dough in bottom and ½ inch up sides of a lightly greased 11- x 7-inch baking dish. Spread jam to edges of dough.

Roll out remaining dough to ¼ inch thickness. Cut dough into ½-inch-wide strips; carefully arrange strips over jam in a lattice design.

Bake at 325° for 36 to 38 minutes or until golden. Cool in pan on a wire rack. Cut into bars. Garnish, if desired. Yield: 15 bars.

CARAMEL-CASHEW SHORTBREAD BARS
Prep: 20 minutes   Cook: 40 minutes

These thick shortbread bars have a crusty, sweet caramel edge. We thought it was yummy.

2 cups all-purpose flour
½ cup sifted powdered sugar
1 cup butter or margarine, cut up
1 (14-ounce) package caramels
    (we tested with Farley's)
⅓ cup whipping cream
½ cup finely chopped unsalted
    cashews

¼ cup all-purpose flour
½ cup uncooked regular oats
¼ cup firmly packed brown sugar
¼ cup finely chopped unsalted
    cashews
⅓ cup butter or margarine, melted

Combine 2 cups flour and powdered sugar in a bowl. Cut 1 cup butter into flour mixture with a pastry blender until mixture is crumbly. Spoon flour mixture into an ungreased 13- x 9-inch baking dish. Press crumb mixture firmly into pan. Bake at 350° for 20 minutes or until shortbread crust is lightly browned.

Melt caramels and whipping cream in a saucepan over medium heat, stirring often. Remove from heat, and stir in ½ cup cashews. Pour over crust in pan.

Combine ¼ cup flour, oats, brown sugar, ¼ cup cashews, and melted butter; stir well. Dollop streusel mixture over caramel in pan, spreading slightly.

Bake at 350° for 20 minutes or until edges are lightly browned. Cool in pan on a wire rack. Cut into bars, using a sharp knife. Yield: 32 bars.

CHEWY APPLE BROWNIES
Prep: 18 minutes   Cook: 1 hour

Enjoy the delicious combination of cinnamon, apple, and nuts with every bite.

2 cups all-purpose flour

1 teaspoon baking soda

1 teaspoon baking powder

1 teaspoon ground cinnamon

½ teaspoon salt

1 cup butter or margarine,
    softened

1¾ cups sugar

2 large eggs

1 teaspoon vanilla extract

2 cups peeled and diced Granny
    Smith apples

½ cup chopped pecans or walnuts

Vanilla ice cream (optional)

Combine first 5 ingredients in a small bowl; set aside.

Beat butter and next 3 ingredients in a large bowl at medium speed with an electric mixer until fluffy.

Gradually stir flour mixture into butter mixture. Stir in apples and pecans. (Mixture will be thick.) Spread dough in a lightly greased 9-inch square pan.

Bake at 350° for 1 hour, shielding with aluminum foil after 35 minutes to prevent excessive browning. Cool in pan on a wire rack. Cut into squares. Serve with ice cream, if desired. Yield: 16 squares.

CAFE-CREAM CHEESE BROWNIES
Prep: 24 minutes   Cook: 45 minutes   Other: 20 minutes

Laced with coffee, these cheese-swirled brownies will please even noncoffee drinkers.

4 (1-ounce) unsweetened
    chocolate baking squares
4 (1-ounce) semisweet chocolate
    baking squares
⅓ cup butter or margarine
1½ tablespoons instant coffee granules
2 tablespoons hot water
2 (3-ounce) packages cream
    cheese, softened
¼ cup butter, softened

2 cups sugar, divided
6 large eggs
1 teaspoon vanilla extract
2 tablespoons all-purpose flour
1½ cups semisweet chocolate
    morsels, divided (9 ounces)
2 teaspoons vanilla extract
1 cup all-purpose flour
1 teaspoon baking powder
1 teaspoon salt

Melt first 3 ingredients in a small saucepan over medium-low heat. Cool. Stir coffee granules into hot water until dissolved. Cool.

Beat cream cheese and ¼ cup butter at medium speed with an electric mixer until creamy; gradually add ½ cup sugar, beating well. Add 2 eggs, 1 at a time, beating until blended. Stir in coffee and 1 teaspoon vanilla. Fold in 2 tablespoons flour and ½ cup chocolate; set cream cheese batter aside.

Beat remaining 4 eggs in a large bowl at medium speed; gradually add remaining 1½ cups sugar, beating well. Add melted chocolate mixture and 2 teaspoons vanilla; beat well. Combine 1 cup flour, baking powder, and salt; fold into chocolate batter. Stir in remaining 1 cup chocolate morsels.

Spread half of chocolate batter in a greased 13- x 9-inch pan. Pour cream cheese batter over chocolate batter. Top with remaining chocolate batter; swirl gently with a knife.

Bake at 325° for 45 minutes (wooden pick will not come out clean). Cool completely in pan on a wire rack. Cut into squares. Yield: 2½ dozen.

Note: Line your pan with aluminum foil to ensure pretty squares and easy cleanup.

DOUBLE CHOCOLATE ESPRESSO BROWNIES

Prep: 20 minutes   Cook: 48 minutes   Other: 2 hours

If you love the rich combination of coffee and chocolate, you'll find these brownies irresistible!

1¼ cups all-purpose flour
¼ teaspoon baking soda
⅛ teaspoon baking powder
⅛ teaspoon salt
14 (1-ounce) semisweet chocolate baking squares, finely chopped (we tested with Baker's)
1 cup sugar
½ cup butter or margarine
¼ cup light corn syrup
¼ cup espresso or strongly brewed French roast coffee
3 large eggs
1 tablespoon vanilla extract
1 cup chopped walnuts
6 ounces premium Swiss dark or milk chocolate, coarsely chopped (we tested with Ghirardelli)

Coat a 13- x 9-inch pan with cooking spray. Line pan with aluminum foil, allowing ends to extend over short sides of pan. Tuck overlapping ends under rim on short sides. Coat foil with cooking spray; set pan aside.

Combine first 4 ingredients in a small bowl. Place chopped semisweet chocolate in a large bowl; set aside.

Combine sugar and next 3 ingredients in a saucepan; cook over medium heat, stirring constantly, until sugar and butter melt and mixture comes to a rolling boil. Remove from heat, and pour over chopped chocolate in bowl; let stand 2 minutes (do not stir). Beat mixture at low speed with an electric mixer until chocolate melts and mixture is smooth. Add eggs, 1 at a time, beating well after each addition. Add flour mixture; beat at medium speed until well blended. Stir in vanilla, walnuts, and dark chocolate.

Spoon batter into prepared pan, spreading evenly. Bake at 325° for 45 to 48 minutes. Cool in pan on a wire rack. Cover brownies with overlapping foil; chill at least 2 hours.

Carefully invert brownies from pan, using overlapping foil as handles; remove foil. Invert brownies again onto a cutting board; cut into squares or diamonds. Yield: 4 dozen.

CHEWY PRALINE-CHOCOLATE FUDGE BARS

Prep: 20 minutes   Cook: 25 minutes

While the bars bake, begin making the rich, nutty icing.

1 cup butter, softened
1 cup firmly packed light brown sugar
1 teaspoon vanilla extract
2 cups all-purpose flour
1 cup chopped pecans, toasted
1 (12-ounce) package semisweet chocolate morsels, divided
Praline Fudge Icing
2 tablespoons milk

Beat butter at medium speed with an electric mixer until creamy; gradually add sugar and vanilla, beating until light and fluffy. Stir in flour and pecans. Press dough evenly into an ungreased 13- x 9-inch baking pan.

Bake at 350° for 20 to 25 minutes or until brown around the edges and cookie mixture pulls away from sides of pan. Sprinkle 1½ cups chocolate morsels evenly over warm cookie mixture. Pour warm Praline Fudge Icing over chocolate morsels; spreading to edges with a spatula.

Microwave remaining ½ cup chocolate morsels and milk in a bowl at HIGH 20 to 30 seconds. Stir until smooth. Drizzle over icing. Cool completely. Cut into bars. Yield: about 7 dozen.

Praline Fudge Icing:

Prep: 10 minutes   Cook: 5 minutes

½ cup butter
1 cup firmly packed light brown sugar
⅛ teaspoon salt
½ cup milk
2½ cups powdered sugar
½ teaspoon vanilla extract
¾ cup chopped pecans, toasted

Melt butter in a saucepan over medium heat. Add brown sugar and salt. Bring to a boil; cook, stirring constantly, 2 minutes. Remove from heat. Stir in milk slowly. Bring to a boil, stirring until smooth. Remove from heat; let stand 5 minutes. Add powdered sugar and vanilla; beat at medium speed with a handheld electric mixer until smooth. Stir in pecans. Yield: about 2 cups.

CHOCOLATE-ORANGE CREAM FINGERS

Prep: 12 minutes   Cook: 22 minutes

We spiked these brownies with orange liqueur, but you can use orange extract.

4 large eggs
2 cups sugar
1 cup all-purpose flour
1 cup unsweetened cocoa
1 cup butter or margarine, melted
1½ teaspoons orange liqueur or
    ½ teaspoon orange extract

3 (1-ounce) unsweetened
    chocolate baking squares
3 tablespoons butter or margarine
Orange Cream Frosting

Beat eggs with a wire whisk until thick and frothy. Add sugar, and stir well. Combine flour and cocoa; gradually stir into egg mixture. Stir in 1 cup melted butter and liqueur. Pour batter into a greased 15- x 10-inch jellyroll pan.

Bake at 350° for 20 to 22 minutes or until a wooden pick inserted in center comes out clean. Cool in pan on a wire rack.

Heat chocolate squares and 3 tablespoons butter in a saucepan over low heat, stirring occasionally. Set aside to cool.

Spread Orange Cream Frosting over uncut brownies. Drizzle cooled chocolate mixture over frosting. Dip a small spatula in hot water, and wipe dry. Using warm spatula, spread chocolate mixture thinly to cover frosting completely. Let stand until

chocolate is set. Cut into thin bars. Store in refrigerator. Yield: 4 dozen.

Orange Cream Frosting:

Prep: 5 minutes

¼ cup butter or margarine, softened
2¾ cups sifted powdered sugar
1 teaspoon grated orange rind
1½ tablespoons fresh orange juice
1 tablespoon orange liqueur or
    1 tablespoon orange juice

Beat butter at medium speed with an electric mixer until creamy; gradually add powdered sugar, beating well. Add rind, 1½ tablespoons juice, and liqueur; beat until blended. Yield: 1¼ cups.

TOFFEE CHEESECAKE BARS

Prep: 16 minutes   Cook: 40 minutes   Other: 8 hours

Cheesecake you can eat with your fingers—that's decadence!

⅔ cup butter or margarine,
    softened
¾ cup firmly packed brown sugar
2 cups all-purpose flour
½ cup chopped pecans
2 (8-ounce) packages cream
    cheese, softened

¾ cup granulated sugar
2 large eggs
1 tablespoon lemon juice
2 teaspoons vanilla extract
1 (7-ounce) package hard toffee
    candies (1 cup), crushed*

Beat butter at medium speed with an electric mixer until creamy; gradually add brown sugar, beating well. Add flour, beating well; stir in pecans. Set aside 1 cup flour mixture. Press remaining flour mixture into a greased 13- x 9-inch pan. Bake at 350° for 14 to 15 minutes or until lightly browned. Remove from oven, and set aside.

Beat cream cheese at medium speed until smooth. Gradually add granulated sugar, beating until mixture is light and fluffy. Add eggs, 1 at a time, beating just until blended. Stir in lemon juice and vanilla.

Pour cream cheese mixture over crust. Sprinkle reserved flour mixture evenly over batter. Bake at 350° for 25 minutes. (Mixture may not be completely set; it will become firm when chilled.) Sprinkle immediately with crushed candies. Cool to room temperature in pan on a wire rack. Cover and chill 8 hours. Cut into bars. Yield: 3 dozen.

*For toffee candies, we used Werther's. Find them on the candy aisle at a local drug store. While crust bakes, crush candies in a large zip-top freezer bag, using a rolling pin.

CHOCOLATE TOFFEE BARS

Prep: 11 minutes   Cook: 35 minutes

Everything that's layered in this bar cookie is yummy.

½ cup butter or margarine, melted
1¾ cups crushed teddy bear-shaped
       chocolate graham cracker
       cookies
1¼ cups toffee bits
6   (1.4-ounce) English toffee candy
       bars, crushed

1   (6-ounce) package semisweet
       chocolate morsels (1 cup)
1   cup chopped pecans
½ cup chopped walnuts
1   (14-ounce) can sweetened
       condensed milk

Line a 13- x 9-inch pan with aluminum foil, allowing foil to extend over ends of pan. Pour melted butter into pan. Sprinkle chocolate crumbs in pan; press firmly, and bake at 325° for 5 minutes.

Layer toffee bits and next 4 ingredients over crust in pan. Press layers down firmly. Pour condensed milk over nuts.

Bake at 325° for 30 minutes or until edges are lightly browned. Cool completely in pan. Lift foil out of pan. Cut cookie mixture into bars. Yield: 2 dozen.

PEANUT BRITTLE BLONDIES

Prep: 12 minutes   Cook: 25 minutes

Dress up classic blond brownies with peanut brittle.
They're rich, sturdy bars—easy to stack and pack for holiday giving.

1½ cups firmly packed light brown sugar	2½ teaspoons baking powder
¾ cup butter	½ teaspoon salt
2 large eggs	3 cups coarsely crushed peanut brittle (about 14 ounces)
2½ cups all-purpose flour	2 teaspoons vanilla extract

Combine brown sugar and butter in a saucepan over medium heat; heat until butter is melted. Remove from heat. Cool slightly; add eggs, 1 at a time, beating until blended after each addition.

Combine flour, baking powder, and salt in a bowl; stir into brown sugar mixture. Stir in peanut brittle and vanilla. Press into a greased and floured 13- x 9-inch baking dish.

Bake at 350° for 25 minutes or until golden. Cool in dish on a wire rack. Cut into bars. Yield: 2 dozen.

CRUNCHY BUTTERY CHOCOLATE BARS
Prep: 8 minutes   Cook: 6 minutes   Other: 4 hours

Chow mein noodles, peanuts, and candy bar chunks provide lots of crunch.

5 cups canned chow mein noodles
  (8.5 ounces)
1 (12-ounce) can peanuts
6 (2.1-ounce) chocolate-covered
  crispy peanut-buttery candy
  bars, coarsely chopped*

¾ cup sugar
1 cup light corn syrup
¾ cup creamy peanut butter
2 (12-ounce) packages semisweet
  chocolate morsels (4 cups),
  melted

Combine first 3 ingredients in a large bowl.

Combine sugar and corn syrup in a saucepan; cook over medium heat, stirring constantly, 6 minutes or until sugar dissolves. Stir in peanut butter.

Pour peanut butter mixture over noodle mixture, and stir well. Spread mixture in a greased 15- x 10-inch jellyroll pan. Spread melted chocolate over noodle mixture. Let stand 4 hours or until chocolate is firm. Cut into bars. Yield: 40 small bars or 30 large bars.

*For candy bars, we used Butterfinger.

SALTED PEANUT CHEWS

Prep: 14 minutes   Cook: 22 minutes   Other: 1 hour

*Miniature marshmallows and peanut butter morsels make these chewy treats
simply too good to resist.*

1½ cups all-purpose flour

½ teaspoon baking powder

¼ teaspoon baking soda

½ teaspoon salt

⅔ cup firmly packed brown sugar

½ cup butter or margarine,
    softened

2 egg yolks

1 teaspoon vanilla extract

3 cups miniature marshmallows

1 (10-ounce) package peanut
    butter morsels

⅔ cup light corn syrup

¼ cup butter or margarine

2 teaspoons vanilla extract

2 cups crisp rice cereal

2 cups salted roasted peanuts

Combine first 8 ingredients in a large mixing bowl. Beat at low speed with an electric mixer until crumbly. Press in an ungreased 13- x 9-inch pan. Bake at 350° for 12 to 15 minutes or until lightly browned. Immediately sprinkle with marshmallows; bake 1 to 2 more minutes or until marshmallows begin to puff. Cool in pan on a wire rack.

Combine peanut butter morsels, corn syrup, ¼ cup butter, and 2 teaspoons vanilla in a large saucepan; cook over low heat, stirring constantly, until smooth. Remove from heat; stir in cereal and peanuts. Spread cereal mixture over marshmallows. Cover and chill 1 hour or until firm. Cut into bars. Yield: 3 dozen.

CRANBERRY-CARAMEL BARS

Prep: 20 minutes   Cook: 35 minutes

Serve these luscious bars to drop-in guests along with a cup of steaming coffee.

1 cup fresh cranberries
2 tablespoons granulated sugar
2⅓ cups all-purpose flour, divided
½ teaspoon baking soda
2 cups uncooked regular oats
½ cup granulated sugar
½ cup firmly packed light brown
    sugar

1 cup butter or margarine, melted
1 (10-ounce) package chopped
    dates
¾ cup chopped pecans
1 (12-ounce) jar caramel sauce

Stir together cranberries and 2 tablespoons sugar in a small bowl; set aside.

Combine 2 cups flour and next 4 ingredients; stir in melted butter until crumbly. Reserve 1 cup flour mixture. Press remaining mixture into a greased 13- x 9-inch baking dish.

Bake at 350° for 15 minutes. Sprinkle with dates, pecans, and cranberry mixture. Stir together caramel sauce and remaining ⅓ cup flour; spoon over cranberries. Sprinkle with reserved 1 cup flour mixture. Bake 20 more minutes or until lightly browned. Cool in pan on a wire rack. Cut into bars. Yield: 2 dozen.

INDEX

Almonds
- Blondies, White Chocolate-Almond, 106
- Cranberry-Almond Cookies, 93
- Lemon-Almond Cookies, 69

Bars & Squares
- Blondies, Peanut Brittle, 120
- Brownies, Chewy Apple, 111
- Cheesecake Bars, Toffee, 118
- Chocolate
  - Blondies, White Chocolate-Almond, 106
  - Brownies, Cafe-Cream Cheese, 113
  - Brownies, Double Chocolate Espresso, 114
  - Brownies, Fudgy Peppermint Candy, 29
  - Buttery Chocolate Bars, Crunchy, 122
  - Congo Bars, 105
  - Fingers, Chocolate-Orange Cream, 116
  - Fudge Bars, Chewy Praline-Chocolate, 115
  - Fudge Bars, Holiday Candy, 104
  - Toffee Bars, Chocolate, 119
- Cranberry-Caramel Bars, 125
- Lemon-Coconut Bar Cookies, 108
- Linzer Bars, Coconut-Raspberry, 109
- Peanut Chews, Salted, 123
- Shortbread Bars, Caramel-Cashew, 110

Beverages
- Hot Chocolate, 13
- Hot Chocolate Mix, 13
- Hot Cinnamon Cocoa, 12
- Hot Cocoa, Old-Fashioned, 12

Chocolate. *See also* Bars & Squares/Chocolate.
- Backpack Cookies, Santa's, 87
- Black-eyed Susans, 79
- Butter Cookies, Chocolate-Tipped, 78
- Buttercrisp Cookies, 94
- Cake Mix Cookies, Easy, 101
- Chunk Cookies, Heavenly Chocolate, 82
- Coffee Bean Cookies, 98
- Crispy Peanut Butter-Chocolate Treats, 19
- Double Chocolate Chews, 31
- Hot Chocolate, 13
- Hot Chocolate Mix, 13
- Hot Cinnamon Cocoa, 12
- Hot Cocoa, Old-Fashioned, 12
- Neapolitan Cookies, 54
- Oatmeal-Chocolate Chip Cookies, Easy, 21
- Oatmeal-Nut-Chocolate Chip Cookies, 88
- Praline-Chocolate Chip Cookies, Crispy, 91
- Snowballs, Chocolate, 65
- Star Cookies, Chocolate, 40
- Thumbprint Cookies, Chocolate-Apricot, 64
- Turtle Cookies, Peanut Butter-Toffee, 95
- Turtles, Mixed Nut, 97

White Chocolate Dream Cookies, 83
Coconut
- Lemon-Coconut Bar Cookies, 108
- Lemon-Coconut Cookies, 69
- Linzer Bars, Coconut-Raspberry, 109
- Santa Cookies, Easy, 60
Coffee
- Bean Cookies, Coffee, 98
- Brownies, Cafe-Cream Cheese, 113
- Brownies, Double Chocolate Espresso, 114

Drop Cookies
- Backpack Cookies, Santa's, 87
- Buttercrisp Cookies, 94
- Cake Mix Cookies, Easy, 101
- Chocolate Chews, Double, 31
- Chocolate Chunk Cookies, Heavenly, 82
- Coffee Bean Cookies, 98
- Cranberry-Almond Cookies, 93
- Fruitcake Cookies, Old-Fashioned, 100
- Oatmeal-Butterscotch Chippers, 86
- Oatmeal-Butterscotch Chippers, Jumbo, 86
- Oatmeal Cookies, Molasses, 85
- Oatmeal-Nut-Chocolate Chip Cookies, 88
- Orange Slice Cookies, 90
- Praline-Chocolate Chip Cookies, Crispy, 91
- Praline Cookies, Crispy, 91
- Turtle Cookies, Peanut Butter-Toffee, 95
- Turtles, Mixed Nut, 97
- White Chocolate Dream Cookies, 83

Frosting, Glazes, and Icings
- Glaze, 18
- Lemon Glaze, 62
- Orange Cream Frosting, 116
- Praline Fudge Icing, 115
- Royal Icing, 18, 44
Fruit. *See also* Lemon.
- Apple Brownies, Chewy, 111
- Apricot Thumbprint Cookies, Chocolate-, 64
- Cherry Icebox Cookies, 68
- Cherry Lemon Crowns, 62
- Cranberry-Almond Cookies, 93
- Cranberry-Caramel Bars, 125
- Cranberry-Walnut Swirls, 70
- Date Nugget Cookies, 56
- Fruitcake Cookies, Old-Fashioned, 100
- Orange-Date-Nut Cookies, 52
- Raspberry Linzer Bars, Coconut-, 109

Lemon
- Almond Cookies, Lemon-, 69
- Cherry Lemon Crowns, 62
- Coconut Bar Cookies, Lemon-, 108

Coconut Cookies, Lemon-, 69
Glaze, Lemon, 62
Icebox Cookies, Lemon, 69
Pecan Cookies, Lemon-, 69
Poppy Seed Cookies, Lemon-, 69

Nuts. *See also* Pecans.
Chocolate Bars, Crunchy Buttery, 122
Congo Bars, 105
Date Nugget Cookies, 56
Hazelnut Crinkle Cookies, 61
Peanut Brittle Blondies, 120
Peanut Chews, Salted, 123
Shortbread Bars, Caramel-Cashew, 110
Turtles, Mixed Nut, 97
Walnut Swirls, Cranberry-, 70

Oatmeal
Buttercrisp Cookies, 94
Chippers, Jumbo Oatmeal-Butterscotch, 86
Chippers, Oatmeal-Butterscotch, 86
Chocolate Chip Cookies, Easy Oatmeal-, 21
Cranberry-Caramel Bars, 125
Fudge Bars, Holiday Candy, 104
Molasses Oatmeal Cookies, 85
Nut-Chocolate Chip Cookies, Oatmeal-, 88
Orange Slice Cookies, 90
Slice-and-Bake Oatmeal Cookies, 72

Pecans. *See also* Nuts.
Butter Cookies, Pecan-, 55
Lemon-Pecan Cookies, 69
Oatmeal-Nut-Chocolate Chip Cookies, 88
Orange-Date-Nut Cookies, 52
Praline-Chocolate Chip Cookies, Crispy, 91
Praline-Chocolate Fudge Bars, Chewy, 115
Praline Cookies, Crispy, 91
Rum Balls, 57

Shaped Cookies
Balls, Rum, 57
Black-eyed Susans, 79
Braided Candy Canes, 14
Butter Cookies, Chocolate-Tipped, 78
Butter Cookies, Melt-away, 78
Cherry Lemon Crowns, 62
Cinnamon Cookies, 49
Crinkle Cookies, Hazelnut, 61
Crispy Peanut-Butter Chocolate Treats, 19
Date Nugget Cookies, 56
Gingerbread People Cookies, 10
Gingerbread Snowflake Cookies, 44
Ginger Cookies, Double, 59
Icebox Cookies, Cherry, 68

Icebox Cookies, Lemon, 69
Jam Kolaches, 42
Lemon-Almond Cookies, 69
Lemon-Coconut Cookies, 69
Lemon-Pecan Cookies, 69
Lemon-Poppy Seed Cookies, 69
Madeleines, Spiced, 67
Neapolitan Cookies, 54
Oatmeal-Chocolate Chip Cookies,
    Easy, 21
Oatmeal Cookies, Slice-and-Bake, 72
Orange-Date-Nut Cookies, 52
Pecan-Butter Cookies, 55
Peppermint Patties, 74
Pfeffernüesse, 76
Santa Cookies, Easy, 60
Shortbread, Basic, 23
Shortbread Cookies, Rosemary, 47
Shortbread, Peppermint Candy, 51
Slice-and-Bake Cookies, Vanilla, 73
Snowballs, Chocolate, 65
Speculaas, 43
Spice Cookies, Slice of, 73
Star Cookies, Chocolate, 40
Sugar Cookies, Brown, 48
Sugar Cookies, Glazed, 18
Sugar Cookies, Sour Cream-Nutmeg, 39
Sugar Crinkles, 30
Sugar Wafers, Christmas, 38
Swirls, Cranberry-Walnut, 70
Tea Cakes, Aunt Neal's Old-Fashioned, 28
Thumbprint Cookies, Chocolate-Apricot, 64
Sugar Cookies
Brown Sugar Cookies, 48
Christmas Sugar Wafers, 38
Crinkles, Sugar, 30
Glazed Sugar Cookies, 18
Sour Cream-Nutmeg Sugar Cookies, 39

Tips
Baking Hints, 32-34
Baking with Kids in the Kitchen, 9
Cookie Cutters, 33-35
Cookie Cutters, Decorative Uses
    for, 34-35
Dough, Chilling, 33
Dough, Rolling, 33
Drop Cookies, Making, 34
Measuring Ingredients, 32-33
Packaging Cookies, 25-27
Primer, Cookie, 32-35
Storing Cookies, 35
Sugar, Coloring, 35
Swap, Cookie, 16-17

Peanut Butter-Toffee
Turtle Cookies
(page 95)